Editors' Acknowledgments

Over the years, we had a dream, nurtured by the ocean, to bring out a book of The Word from New Jersey. Our dream has taken root in reality, and we have many people to thank: X. J. Kennedy, who wrote the perceptive Introduction to the book, and who, in his poetical wisdom, helped us conceive a title; Stephen Dunn, who in his spirited Foreword identifies New Jersey's unique poetic situation; Lorin Rizco, our typist and best friend, the professional keel to our ship, faithfully typing and retyping the manuscript and encouraging us; George Valente, our publisher, taking a risk in publishing the book, saintly in giving Life to the Word; Ron at Ron's West End Pub, in whose Inn we spent hours and hours planning the book, choosing and unchoosing poets and poems; the poets themselves, the lyrical stream.

CONTENTS

CONTENTS

FOREWORD

I doubt that there's another anthology—defined by state or region—as multi-voiced and yet as agenda free as this one. The editors did not attempt to make their selections thematic, or reflective of a vision they had of New Jersey. No doubt they knew New Jersey too well for that; the state—with its multitudes, its smokestacks and rolling hills—would have defeated them. Instead, they were interested in the poetry New Jersey poets have written, whether New Jersey oriented or not. They'd let the art itself, therefore, be its own representation—literally, the art of the state. That some of the poets included are among America's finest must have inspired in them an early confidence.

Yet most of the poems testify that New Jersey has been a place that has freed its poets of place. No historical wound to exert pressure on our imaginations, as there might be, say, in Virginia or Georgia. No idiosyncratic blend of Puritanism and individualism in states like Massachusetts and New Hampshire, no idiom peculiar to a collective ethos. Lacking a clear identity, New Jersey has allowed its poets to be in and of their environment yet at the same time liberated from any need of addressing some overarching sense of it. Truth be told, no poet worth his or her mettle wants to be defined solely by region, no less by state. For the most part, the poets included here don't speak New Jersey. They speak from it.

X. J. Kennedy, in his excellent Introduction, claims quite accurately that New Jersey's cultural and geographical diversity is "a mishmash that never got unified." He as easily could have been speaking about our emotional lives. A mishmash might be bad for accountants, but we know that poets often thrive amid such confusion. And indeed this anthology proves that they have. The poets included here are a varied bunch, from well known to unknown, and their poems evoke the immediacies of lives lived and unlived, the manifest world and the concealed world, all the normal stuff of poetry. When they do set their poems in New Jersey's complex urban, rural, and suburban terrain, one thing is clear: a New Jersey poet knows that the beautiful is never very far from the tawdry.

As one of those New Jersey poets, let me add something personal. I'd lived for twenty years in South Jersey when one day I realized that almost all of my "landscapes" were psychological, that in my poems I'd rarely taken on the place where I lived. In succeeding books I attempted to correct that. In one poem, in answer to a student's question about why I hadn't left South Jersey, the surrogate I who is me says, "Because it hasn't been invented yet." I would extend that to New Jersey itself. It remains a literary opportunity. Which is not to say that any particular poet should seize it. New Jersey's gift to its poets, as I've suggested, is that it's a place of many places, essentially amorphous, freeing us to look at the world.

— *Stephen Dunn*

INTRODUCTION

Image and Actuality

Henry Miller once pictured himself standing on the New York waterfront gazing over to the relatively dark shore across the Hudson and saying of New Jersey, "How could anything great ever come from there?" This dismissal recalls the disparaging view of New Jersey you customarily hear from people who think the state nothing but a polluted stretch of turnpike between Manhattan and Philadelphia.

Nor has the shape of New Jersey on the map, like that of a big-nosed little old lady wearing a flat hat, helped the state's image. A poet named Jack Anderson once printed a poem (naturally, in a New York magazine) called "The Invention of New Jersey," summing up the territory in a vision of swamps, refineries, plastic geegaws, and neon hot-dog signs, where on a weekend a man has nothing to do but aimlessly drive around and have sex with his sour-faced date. Like Miller, such commentators ignore far more than they know.

New Jersey, let's admit, is a mishmash that never got unified.

By its geographical situation it has always been a crossroads, a place for people to commute from, for Revolutionary armies to pass through. This makes any general idea of it difficult to grasp. Its proximity to Manhattan has proved both an advantage and, for its culture, an inhibiting force. Why found a world-class art museum in New Jersey with the Metropolitan and the MOMA so close by? Regional theater has had stiff competition from Broadway, Off-Broadway, and Off-Off-Broadway, although among other companies Amiri Baraka's Spirit House Theater, the Paper Mill and George Street Playhouses, the Crossroads and McCarter Theatres, and the New Jersey Shakespeare Festival have managed to achieve distinction. Still, unlike France, New Jersey has no Paris; unlike Illinois, no Chicago; unlike Georgia, no Atlanta—no focal point for art and commerce and literature. Once, in my Dover boyhood, Newark aspired to being such a center, with the corner of Broad and Market for its bustling Etoile or Loop and its influential *Newark Evening News* circulating statewide. But urban blight and riots caused the city to dwindle in importance. Nowadays it is the site of one of three big metropolitan airports, a jumping-off-place for travelers heading overseas.

Has New Jersey a common language? I daresay a native of Jersey City and a South Jersey tomato farmer can understand each other, but just barely.

Is there a common culture? Ask a Passaic slum-dweller how much kinship he feels to the owner of a Princeton estate, where, it is rumored, the servants are direct descendants of the family's original slaves. New Jersey is a land of stark contrasts and furious contradictions. From the garbage-heaped swamps of the Meadowlands you can see the Empire State Building. Between the orchards of Essex County and the fuel tanks of Bayonne, between picturesque Cape May or the Delaware Water Gap and the trafficked corridors of the Garden State Parkway (the New Jersey Piedmont has the densest population in the USA), between the Appalachians to the north and the flat farmlands to the south, between the mean streets of Atlantic City and the glitzy casinos they hide behind, there isn't much vital relationship.

And yet out of this stopping-place, this fervent and fruitful confusion, out of Edison's Menlo Park laboratory and the Wright Aeronautics factory, have come forces to transform the world. Not all of these changes have been technological. From Hoboken, Frank Sinatra remade the nature of pop singing and from Asbury Park, Bruce Springsteen has worked an ongoing transformation in pop music. From Camden, Walt Whitman spread his influence and indeed began modern American poetry; from Newark, Stephen Crane showed that it could be written with concision; and from Paterson, William Carlos Williams proved that its speech could be taken "out of the mouths of Polish mothers." Allen Ginsberg, for whom Williams served as baby doctor, carried on this literary revolution. Without New Jersey, the world today would be darker and quieter; and contemporary American poetry, inconceivable.

In their historical anthology of New Jersey poets, Emanuel di Pasquale, Frank Finale, and Sander Zulauf set out bravely to widen blinkered perspectives. The achievements of Whitman, Crane, and Williams ought to be enough to wise up a legion of Henry Millers, or literary turnpike travelers. Yet this anthology goes far deeper, as the most cursory browse through it will show. The blue roads and byways of New Jersey are heavily populated by poets whom any state might wish to claim for its laureates. Some of the poets here included are natives like Williams, who stayed put in Rutherford for practically all his life; some are transplants like Whitman, who though he grew up on Long Island and learned to orate his long lines by howling them to its crashing waves, did after all live in Camden for his last twenty years, there retooling his *Leaves of Grass* into its final version. Other poets merely passed through for a short time and moved on, as did Marianne Moore. But the editors have reason to feel that these transients, too, left their mark and deserve to be represented. As a result, the reader is in for some surprises: What?—that naturalized Irishman Paul Muldoon a New Jersey poet? But until Princeton secedes from the Garden State, let us count him in. Some of these poems have New Jersey written all over them—like "The Puritan's Ballad" of Elinor Wylie, in which we are startled to find romantic use of a familiar New Jersey name ("My love came up from Barnegat"), Robert Pinsky's "Jersey Rain," Thomas Reiter's "Going into the Barrens," Stephen Dunn's "The Metaphysicians of South Jersey," and more. Other poems do not advertise their New Jersey connections and arguably might have been written anywhere. The editors don't fall into the trap of confining these poets to New Jersey land-scapes. They rightly include "Supermarket in California," considering it one of Allen Ginsberg's best poems.

Like more than half of all Americans, I am now relocated and deracin-ated, and so find it a wondrous lift to read this exciting, immensely various anthology and feel again some New Jersey connections. Not that you have to be from New Jersey, or still living there, to discover in this book a splendid and eye-opening read. Throw away your preconceptions and plunge in. Let yourself soar beyond that Manhattan-to-Philadelphia corridor.

— X. J. Kennedy

EDITORIAL NOTE

We wanted to celebrate the essential voices of the extraordinary poets who have lived and worked in New Jersey, from the earliest times to the present. We wanted to gather a collection of poems which danced to the unique rhythms and music of New Jersey, not the gritty industrial darkness and ugly bitterness that regularly represent New Jersey in so many other artistic venues. We wanted to reach back to the earlier poets—the Revolutionary War "Father of American Poetry" from Freehold (Freneau), the "revolutionizer" of poetry from Camden (Whitman), the poet who bridged the realists to the moderns from Newark (Crane), and three key figures of modernism (Williams in Rutherford, Moore in Chatham, and Burke in Andover), their direct descendants, the poets of the Beat Generation, Ginsberg (Paterson) and Baraka (Newark), and our current Pulitzer Prize poets, Komunyakaa, C. K. Williams, Muldoon (Princeton), and Dunn (Stockton)—and gather the poetic greatness distilled from life in this state in one place.

What Wordsworth and Coleridge did for poetry in their 1798 *Lyrical Ballads,* we wanted to do for poetry at the dawn of the 21st century—not with our own voices, as they did, writing a manifesto of Romanticism intent on burying the Classical Age, but instead a collection of poems that reveals the emotional honesty required to live here. Our criterion was simple: we wanted to hear the pure, clear words of the poets who have called this place home. We were not looking for poems about New Jersey, although there are plenty of them in this book. We did not want the rumble and thunder and big dramatic crescendos of Wagner, but the wondrous tenderness and generosity of Puccini. New Jersey has plenty of the former shouting in its streets and roaring down its highway corridors every day, and not enough mirroring the latter, the true, nourishing home-cooked food for the soul that keeps us all alive together and talking to each other, day by day. Our hope is that you find the spirit of the place in these diverse voices and visions.

— Emanuel di Pasquale, Frank Finale, and Sander Zulauf

THE
POETS
OF
NEW JERSEY

PHILIP FRENEAU

(1752 – 1832)

☙

*"The Father of American Poetry," a Princeton graduate known for his patri-
otic and political poems, which were mildly praised by George Washington
(who dubbed him a "rascal") and admired by Thomas Jefferson. A man of
many talents and vocations, he lived his last thirty years in relative obscurity
on his farm near Freehold in Monmouth County writing lyrics celebrating
life in the new republic.*

The Indian Burying Ground

*"The North American Indians bury their dead in a sitting posture; decorating
the corpse with wampum, the images of birds, quadrupeds, &c. And (if that of
a warrior) with bows, arrows, tomahawks, and other military weapons."*

—Freneau

In spite of all the learned have said,
    I still my old opinion keep;
The posture, that we give the dead,
    Points out the soul's eternal sleep.

Not so the ancients of these lands—
    The Indian, when from life released,
Again is seated with his friends,
    And shares again the joyous feast.

His imaged birds, and painted bowl,
    And venison, for a journey dressed,
Bespeak the nature of the soul,
    Activity, that knows no rest.

His bow, for action ready bent,
  And arrows, with a head of stone,
Can only mean that life is spent,
  And not the old ideas gone.

Thou, stranger, that shalt come this way,
  No fraud upon the dead commit—
Observe the swelling turf, and say
  They do not lie, but here they sit.

Here still a lofty rock remains,
  On which the curious eye may trace
(Now wasted, half, by wearing rains)
  The fancies of a ruder race.

Here still an aged elm aspires,
  Beneath whose far-projecting shade
(And which the shepherd still admires)
  The children of the forest played!

There oft a restless Indian queen
  (Pale Shebah, with her braided hair)
And many a barbarous form is seen
  To chide the man that lingers there.

By midnight moons, o'er moistening dews;
  In habit for the chase arrayed,
The hunter still the deer pursues,
  The hunter and the deer, a shade!

And long shall timorous fancy see
  The painted chief, and pointed spear,
And Reason's self shall bow the knee
  To shadows and delusions here.

The Wild Honey Suckle

Fair flower, that dost so comely grow,
Hid in this silent dull retreat,
Untouch'd thy honey'd blossoms blow;
Unseen thy little branches greet:
    No roving foot shall find thee here,
    No busy hand provoke a tear.

By nature's self in white array'd,
She bade thee shun the vulgar eye,
And planted here the guardian shade,
And sent soft waters murmuring by;
    Thus quietly thy summer goes,
    Thy days declining to repose.

Smit with these charms, that must decay,
I grieve to see thy future doom;
They died—nor were those flowers less gay,
(The flowers that did in Eden bloom)
    Unpitying frosts and Autumn's power
    Shall leave no vestige of this flower.

From morning suns and evening dews
At first, thy little being came:
If nothing once, you nothing lose,
For when you die, you are the same;
    The space between is but an hour,
    The frail duration of a flower.

WALT WHITMAN

(1819 – 1892)

∞

Published Leaves of Grass *in 1855, and added poems to each of the eight subsequent editions printed during his lifetime. Whitman and Emily Dickinson are generally acknowledged to be the two greatest poets America has produced. He lived on Mickle Street in Camden from 1873 until his death.*

from Song of Myself

1

I celebrate myself, and sing myself,
And what I assume you shall assume,
For every atom belonging to me as good belongs to you.

I loafe and invite my soul,
I lean and loafe at my ease observing a spear of summer grass.

My tongue, every atom of my blood, form'd from this soil, this air;
Born here of parents born here from parents the same, and their
    parents the same,
I, now thirty-seven years old in perfect health begin,
Hoping to cease not till death.

Creeds and schools in abeyance,
Retiring back a while sufficed at what they are, but never forgotten,
I harbor for good or bad, I permit to speak at every hazard,
Nature without check with original energy.

6

A child said *What is the grass?* Fetching it to me with full hands;
How could I answer the child? I do not know what it is any more
      than he.
I guess it must be the flag of my disposition, out of hopeful
      green stuff woven.

Or I guess it is the handkerchief of the Lord,
A scented gift and remembrancer designedly dropt,
Bearing the owner's name someway in the corners, that we may see
      and remark, and say *Whose?*

Or I guess the grass is itself a child, the produced babe of
      the vegetation.

Or I guess it is a uniform hieroglyphic,
And it means, Sprouting alike in broad zones and narrow zones,
Growing among black folks as among white,
Kanuck, Tuckahoe, Congressman, Cuff, I give them the same,
      I receive them the same.

And now it seems to me the beautiful uncut hair of graves.

Tenderly will I use you curling grass,
It may be you transpire from the breasts of young men,
It may be if I had known them I would have loved them,
It may be you are from old people, or from offspring taken
      soon out of their mothers' laps,
And here you are the mothers' laps.

This grass is very dark to be from the white heads of old mothers,
Darker than the colorless beards of old men,
Dark to come from under the faint red roofs of mouths.

O I perceive after all so many uttering tongues,
And I perceive they do not come from the roofs of mouths
    for nothing.

I wish I could translate the hints about the dead young men
    and women,
And the hints about old men and mothers, and the offspring
    taken soon out of their laps.

What do you think has become of the young and old men?
And what do you think has become of the women and children?

They are alive and well somewhere,
The smallest sprout shows there is really no death,
And if ever there was it led forward life, and does not wait
    at the end to arrest it,
And ceas'd the moment life appear'd.

All goes onward and outward, nothing collapses,
And to die is different from what any one supposed, and luckier.

31

I believe a leaf of grass is no less than the journey-work of the stars,
And the pismire is equally perfect, and a grain of sand, and the egg
    of the wren,
And the tree-toad is a chef-d'oeuvre for the highest,
And the running blackberry would adorn the parlors of heaven,
And the narrowest hinge in my hand puts to scorn all machinery,
And the cow crunching with depress'd head surpasses any statue,
And a mouse is miracle enough to stagger sextillions of infidels.

I find I incorporate gneiss, coal, long-threaded moss, fruits, grains,
    esculent roots,
And am stucco'd with quadrupeds and birds all over,
And have distanced what is behind me for good reasons,
But call any thing back again when I desire it.
In vain the speeding or shyness,
In vain the plutonic rocks send their old heat against my approach,
In vain the mastodon retreats beneath its own powder'd bones,
In vain objects stand leagues off and assume manifold shapes,
In vain the ocean settling in hollows and the great monsters
    lying low,
In vain the buzzard houses herself with the sky,
In vain the snake slides through the creepers and logs,
In vain the elk takes to the inner passes of the woods,
In vain the razor-bill'd auk sails far north to Labrador,
I follow quickly, I ascend to the nest in the fissure of the cliff.

48

I have said that the soul is not more than the body,
And I have said that the body is not more than the soul,
And nothing, not God, is greater to one than one's self is,
And whoever walks a furlong without sympathy walks to his
    own funeral drest in his shroud,
And I or you pocketless of a dime may purchase the pick of the earth,
And to glance with an eye or show a bean in its pod
    confounds the learning of all times,
And there is no trade or employment but the young man following it
    may become a hero,
And there is no object so soft but it makes a hub for the
    wheel'd universe,
And I say to any man or woman, Let your soul stand cool
    and composed before a million universes.

And I say to mankind, Be not curious about God,
For I who am curious about each am not curious about God,
(No array of terms can say how much I am at peace about God
    and about death.)

I hear and behold God in every object, yet understand God not in
    the least,
Nor do I understand who there can be more wonderful than myself.

Why should I wish to see God better than this day?
I see something of God each hour of the twenty-four, and each
    moment then,
In the faces of men and women I see God, and in my own face
    in the glass,
I find letters from God dropt in the street, and every one is sign'd
    by God's name,
And I leave them where they are, for I know that wheresoe'er I go,
Others will punctually come for ever and ever.

49

And as to you Death, and you bitter hug of mortality, it is idle to try
    to alarm me.

To his work without flinching the accoucheur comes,
I see the elder-hand pressing receiving supporting,
I recline by the sills of the exquisite flexible doors,
And mark the outlet, and mark the relief and escape.

And as to you Corpse I think you are good manure, but that does not
    offend me,
I smell the white roses sweet-scented and growing,
I reach to the leafy lips, I reach to the polish'd breasts of melons.

And as to you Life I reckon you are the leavings of many deaths,
(No doubt I have died myself ten thousand times before.)

I hear you whispering there O stars of heaven,
O suns—O grass of graves—O perpetual transfers and promotions,
If you do not say any thing how can I say any thing?

Of the turbid pool that lies in the autumn forest,
Of the moon that descends the steeps of the soughing twilight,
Toss, sparkles of day and dusk—toss on the black stems that decay
    in the muck,
Toss to the moaning gibberish of the dry limbs.

I ascend from the moon, I ascend from the night,
I perceive that the ghastly glimmer is noonday sunbeams reflected,
And debouch to the steady and central from the offspring
    great or small.

50

There is that in me—I do not know what it is—but I know it is in me.

Wrench'd and sweaty—calm and cool then my body becomes,
I sleep—I sleep long.

I do not know it—it is without name—it is a word unsaid,
It is not in any dictionary, utterance, symbol.

Something it swings on more than the earth I swing on,
To it the creation is the friend whose embracing awakes me.

Perhaps I might tell more. Outlines! I plead for my brothers
    and sisters.

Do you see O my brothers and sisters?
It is not chaos or death—it is form, union, plan—it is eternal life—
    it is Happiness.

51

The past and present wilt—I have fill'd them, emptied them,
And proceed to fill my next fold of the future.

Listener up there! What have you to confide to me?
Look in my face while I snuff the sidle of evening,
(Talk honestly, no one else hears you, and I stay only a
    minute longer.)

Do I contradict myself?
Very well then I contradict myself,
(I am large, I contain multitudes.)
I concentrate toward them that are nigh, I wait on the door-slab.

Who had done his day's work? Who will soonest be through
    with his supper?
Who wishes to walk with me?

Will you speak before I am gone? Will you prove already too late?

52

The spotted hawk swoops by and accuses me, he complains of my
gab and my loitering.

I too am not a bit tamed, I too am untranslatable,
I sound my barbaric yawp over the roofs of the world.

The last scud of day holds back for me,
It flings my likeness after the rest and true as any on the
shadow'd wilds,
It coaxes me to the vapor and the dusk.

I depart as air, I shake my white locks at the runaway sun,
I effuse my flesh in eddies, and drift it in lacy jags.

I bequeath myself to the dirt to grow from the grass I love,
If you want me again look for me under your boot-soles.

You will hardly know who I am or what I mean,
But I shall be good health to you nevertheless,
And filter and fibre your blood.

Failing to fetch me at first keep encouraged,
Missing me one place search another,
I stop somewhere waiting for you.

Roaming in Thought
(After reading Hegel.*)*

Roaming in thought over the Universe, I saw the little that
    is Good steadily hastening towards immortality,
And the vast all that is call'd Evil I saw hastening to merge
    itself and become lost and dead.

A Farm Picture

Through the ample open door of the peaceful country barn
A sunlit pasture field with cattle and horses feeding,
And haze and vista, and the far horizon fading away.

A Child's Amaze

Silent and amazed even when a little boy,
I remember I heard the preacher every Sunday put God in
    his statements,
As contending against some being or influence.

The Runner

On a flat road runs the well-train'd runner,
He is lean and sinewy with muscular legs,
He is thinly clothed, he leans forward as he runs,
With lightly closed fists and arms partially rais'd.

Beautiful Women

Women sit or move to and fro, some old, some young,
The young are beautiful—but the old are more beautiful
than the young.

Mother and Babe

I see the sleeping babe nestling the breast of its mother,
The sleeping mother and babe—hush'd, I study them long
and long.

Thought

Of obedience, faith, adhesiveness;
As I stand aloof and look there is to me something
profoundly affecting in large masses of men following
the lead of those who do not believe in men.

Visor'd

A mask, a perpetual natural disguiser of herself,
Concealing her face, concealing her form,
Changes and transformations every hour, every moment,
Falling upon her even when she sleeps.

Thought

Of Justice—as if Justice could be any thing but the same
    ample law, expounded by natural judges and saviors,
As if it might be this thing or that thing, according to decisions.

A Noiseless Patient Spider

A noiseless patient spider,
I mark'd where on a little promontory it stood isolated,
Mark'd how to explore the vacant vast surrounding,
It launch'd forth filament, filament, filament, out of itself,
Ever unreeling them, ever tirelessly speeding them.

And you O my soul where you stand,
Surrounded, detached, in measureless oceans of space,
Ceaselessly musing, venturing, throwing, seeking the spheres
    to connect them,
Till the bridge you will need be form'd, till the ductile anchor hold,
Till the gossamer thread you fling catch somewhere, O my soul.

from **Fancies at Navesink: Had I the Choice**

Had I the choice to tally greatest bards,
To limn their portraits, stately, beautiful, and emulate at will,
Homer with all his wars and warriors—Hector, Achilles, Ajax,
Or Shakespere's woe-entangled Hamlet, Lear, Othello—
    Tennyson's fair ladies,
Metre or wit the best, or choice conceit to wield in perfect rhyme,
    delight of singers;
These, these, O sea, all these I'd gladly barter,
Would you the undulation of one wave, its trick to me transfer,
Or breathe one breath of yours upon my verse,
And leave its odor there.

Locusts and Katydids

Aug. 22.—Reedy monotones of locust, or sounds of katy-did—I hear the latter at night, and the other both day and night. I thought the morning and evening warble of birds delightful; but I find I can listen to these strange insects with just as much pleasure. A single locust is now heard near noon from a tree two hundred feet off, as I write—a long whirring, continued, quite loud noise graded in distinct whirls, or swinging circles, increasing in strength and rapidity up to a certain point, and then a fluttering, quietly tapering fall. Each strain is continued from one to two minutes. The locust-song is very appropriate to the scene—gushes, has meaning, is masculine, is like some fine old wine, not sweet, but far better than sweet.

But the katydid—how shall I describe its piquant utter-ances? One sings from a willow-tree just outside my open bedroom window, twenty yards distant; every clear night for a fortnight past has sooth'd me to sleep. I rode through a piece of woods for a hundred rods the other evening, and heard the katydids by myriads—very curious for once; but I like better my single neighbor on the tree.

Let me say more about the song of the locust, even to rep-etition; a long, chromatic, tremulous crescendo, like a brass disk whirling round and round, emitting wave after wave of notes, beginning with a certain moderate beat or measure, rapidly increasing in speed and emphasis, reaching a point of great energy and significance, and then quickly and gracefully dropping down and out. Not the melody of the swinging-bird—far from it; the common musician might think without melody, but surely having to the finer ear a harmony of its own; monotonous—but what a swing there is in that brassy drone, round and round, cymballine—or like the whirling of brass quoits.

STEPHEN CRANE
(1871 – 1900)

∞

He was born in Newark and lived in Asbury Park and Port Jervis, NY. He wrote the great novel of the American civil war, The Red Badge of Courage *(1895), without ever seeing a battle. That same year he published his first volume of poems,* The Black Riders, *followed by many short stories, novels, and a second volume of poetry,* War Is Kind *(1899).*

from The Black Riders

III

In the desert
I saw a creature, naked, bestial,
Who, squatting upon the ground,
Held his heart in his hands,
And ate of it.
I said, "Is it good, friend?"
"It is bitter—bitter," he answered;
"But I like it
Because it is bitter,
And because it is my heart."

from **Intrigue**

X

I have seen thy face aflame
For love of me,
Thy fair arms go mad,
Thy lips tremble and mutter and rave.
And—surely—
This should leave a man content?
Thou lovest not me now,
But thou didst love me,
And in loving me once
Thou gavest me an eternal privilege,
For I can think of thee.

from **War Is Kind**

XXI

A man said to the universe:
"Sir, I exist!"
"However," replied the universe,
"The fact has not created in me
A sense of obligation."

from **The Black Riders**

XXIV

I saw a man pursuing the horizon;
Round and round they sped.
I was disturbed at this;
I accosted the man.
"It is futile," I said,
"You can never—"

"You lie," he cried,
And ran on.

WILLIAM CARLOS WILLIAMS

(1883 – 1963)

ᗧ

An obstetrician, Dr. Williams lived and practiced in Rutherford where he wrote his poems, short stories, and essays. One of the founders of modern American poetry, in the 1940's he wrote Paterson. *He was embraced by the Beat Generation poets (especially Ginsberg, Kerouac, and Corso) as their inspired poetic master.*

To Waken an Old Lady

Old age is
a flight of small
cheeping birds
skimming
bare trees
above a snow glaze.
Gaining and failing
they are buffetted
by a dark wind—
But what?
On harsh weedstalks
the flock has rested,
the snow
is covered with broken
seedhusks
and the wind tempered
by a shrill
piping of plenty.

Spring and All

I

By the road to the contagious hospital
under the surge of the blue
mottled clouds driven from the
northeast—a cold wind. Beyond, the
waste of broad, muddy fields
brown with dried weeds, standing and fallen

patches of standing water
the scattering of tall trees

All along the road the reddish
purplish, forked, upstanding, twiggy
stuff of bushes and small trees
with dead, brown leaves under them
leafless vines—

Lifeless in appearance, sluggish
dazed spring approaches—

They enter the new world naked,
cold, uncertain of all
save that they enter. All about them
the cold, familiar wind—

Now the grass, tomorrow
the stiff curl of wildcarrot leaf

One by one objects are defined—
It quickens: clarity, outline of leaf

But now the stark dignity of
entrance—Still, the profound change
has come upon them: rooted they
grip down and begin to awaken

The Dance

In Breughel's great picture, The Kermess,
the dancers go round, they go round and
around, the squeal and the blare and the
tweedle of bagpipes, a bugle and fiddles
tipping their bellies (round as the thick-
sided glasses whose wash they impound)
their hips and their bellies off balance
to turn them. Kicking and rolling about
the Fair Grounds, swinging their butts, those
shanks must be sound to bear up under such
rollicking measures, prance as they dance
in Breughel's great picture, The Kermess.

Danse Russe

If I when my wife is sleeping
and the baby and Kathleen
are sleeping
and the sun is a flame-white disc
in silken mists
above shining trees,—
if I in my north room
dance naked, grotesquely
before my mirror
waving my shirt round my head
and singing softly to myself:
"I am lonely, lonely.
I was born to be lonely,
I am best so!"
If I admire my arms, my face
my shoulders, flanks, buttocks
against the yellow drawn shades,—

Who shall say I am not
the happy genius of my household?

ELINOR WYLIE

(1885 – 1928)

∞

A lyric poet and novelist, born in New Jersey, she lived in Summit. Her widely popular love poems and other lyrics were collected by her husband, William Rose Benét, and published posthumously in 1932.

The Puritan's Ballad

My love came up from Barnegat,
   The sea was in his eyes;
He trod as softly as a cat
   And told me terrible lies.

His hair was yellow as new-cut pine
   In shavings curled and feathered;
I thought how silver it would shine
   By cruel winters weathered.

But he was in his twentieth year,
   This time I'm speaking of;
We were head over heels in love with fear
   And half a-feared of love.

His feet were used to treading a gale
   And balancing thereon;
His face was brown as a foreign sail
   Threadbare against the sun.

His arms were thick as hickory logs
    Whittled to little wrists;
Strong as the teeth of terrier dogs
    Were the fingers of his fists.

Within his arms I feared to sink
    Where lions shook their manes,
And dragons drawn in azure ink
    Leapt quickened by his veins.

Dreadful his strength and length of limb
    As the sea to foundering ships;
I dipped my hands in love for him
    No deeper than their tips.

But our palms were welded by a flame
    The moment we came to part,
And on his knuckles I read my name
    Enscrolled within a heart.

And something made our wills to bend
    As wild as trees blown over;
We were no longer friend and friend,
    But only lover and lover.

"In seven weeks or seventy years—
    God grant it may be sooner!—
I'll make a handkerchief for your tears
    From the sails of my captain's schooner.

"We'll wear our loves like wedding rings
    Long polished to our touch;
We shall be busy with other things
    And they cannot bother us much.

"When you are skimming the wrinkled cream
    And your ring clinks on the pan,
You'll say to yourself in a pensive dream,
    'How wonderful a man!'

"When I am slitting a fish's head
    And my ring clanks on the knife,
I'll say with thanks, as a prayer is said,
    'How beautiful a wife!'

"And I shall fold my decorous paws
    In velvet smooth and deep,
Like a kitten that covers up its claws
    To sleep and sleep and sleep.

"Like a little blue pigeon you shall bow
    Your bright alarming crest;
In the crook of my arm you'll lay your brow
    To rest and rest and rest."

Will he never come back from Barnegat
    With thunder in his eyes,
Treading as soft as a tiger cat,
    To tell me terrible lies?

JOYCE KILMER

(1886 – 1918)

∞

Lived in Mahwah. His fame is based on his poem "Trees" which was pub-lished in Poetry *in 1913. The celebrated tree became diseased in the early 1960s and was removed from the campus of Rutgers University in New Brunswick. A rest stop on the New Jersey Turnpike is named in honor of this poet who was killed in France in the final weeks of World War I.*

Trees
(For Mrs. Henry Mills Alden)

I think that I shall never see
A poem lovely as a tree.

A tree whose hungry mouth is prest
Against the earth's sweet flowing breast;

A tree that looks at God all day,
And lifts her leafy arms to pray;

A tree that may in summer wear
A nest of robins in her hair;

Upon whose bosom snow has lain;
Who intimately lives with rain.

Poems are made by fools like me,
But only God can make a tree.

MARIANNE MOORE

(1887 – 1972)

∞

A major poet and shaper of modern American poetry, she lived in Chatham before moving to Brooklyn. Her finely crafted lyric stanzas and insightfully precise language made her an extraordinarily influential poet, encouraging younger poets who sought her out, especially Elizabeth Bishop.

The Fish

wade
through black jade.
        Of the crow-blue mussel shells, one keeps
        adjusting the ash heaps;
                opening and shutting itself like

an
injured fan.
        The barnacles which encrust the side
        of the wave, cannot hide
                there for the submerged shafts of the

sun,
split like spun
        glass, move themselves with spotlight swiftness
        into the crevices—
                in and out, illuminating

the
turquoise sea
    of bodies. The water drives a wedge
    of iron through the iron edge
        of the cliff; whereupon the stars,

pink
rice-grains, ink-
    bespattered jellyfish, crabs like green
    lilies, and submarine
        toadstools, slide each on the other.

All
external
    marks of abuse are present on this
    defiant edifice—
        all the physical features of

ac-
cident—lack
    of cornice, dynamite grooves, burns, and
    hatchet strokes, these things stand
        out on it; the chasm side is

dead.
Repeated
    evidence has proved that it can live
    on what can not revive
        its youth. The sea grows old in it.

Poetry

I, too, dislike it: there are things that are important beyond all this fiddle.
    Reading it, however, with a perfect contempt for it, one discovers in
    it after all, a place for the genuine.
        Hands that can grasp, eyes
        that can dilate, hair that can rise
            if it must, these things are important not because a

high-sounding interpretation can be put upon them but because they are
    useful. When they become so derivative as to become unintelligible,
    the same thing may be said for all of us, that we
        do not admire what
        we cannot understand: the bat
            holding on upside down or in quest of something to

eat, elephants pushing, a wild horse taking a roll, a tireless wolf under
    a tree, the immovable critic twitching his skin like a horse that feels
                        a flea, the base-
    ball fan, the statistician—
        nor is it valid
        to discriminate against "business documents and

school-books"; all these phenomena are important. One must make a
                      distinction
    however: when dragged into prominence by half poets, the result
                      is not poetry,
    nor till the poets among us can be
        "literalists of
        the imagination"—above
            insolence and triviality and can present

for inspection, "imaginary gardens with real toads in them," shall we have
   it. In the meantime, if you demand on the one hand,
     the raw material of poetry in
        all its rawness and
        that which is on the other hand
           genuine, you are interested in poetry.

DOROTHY PARKER

(1893 – 1967)

෨

*Born Dorothy Rothschild in the West End section of Long Branch, she pub-
lished her first poem in* Vanity Fair *in 1914. Her poetry, short stories and
drama criticism appeared regularly in* The New Yorker, *and she was the
only female founding member of the famed Algonquin "Round Table."*

Résumé

Razors pain you;
Rivers are damp;
Acids stain you;
And drugs cause cramp.
Guns aren't lawful;
Nooses give;
Gas smells awful;
You might as well live.

News Item

Men seldom make passes
At girls who wear glasses.

LOUIS GINSBERG

(1896 – 1976)

∞

Taught high school English in Paterson. His short, metaphysical lyrics appeared in many newspapers and magazines. Near the end of his life, he reconciled with his son, Allen, and they gave many father-and-son poetry readings together.

Song

I wonder how the buttercup
    Is gathering its trust
And how the crocus syphons up
    Its daring from the dust.

I think what meaning flows above
    The earth so it can fill
The lovely exclamation of
    A yellow daffodil.

And yet is it enough for me
    to watch the flowers come
And muse upon the mystery
    That they are growing from.

KENNETH BURKE

(1897 – 1993)

∞

Lived in Byram Township. He became one of America's leading philoso-
phers of language in the 20th century, with such works as Attitudes Toward
History, A Grammar of Motives, A Rhetoric of Motives, Language as
Symbolic Action, *and* The Philosophy of Literary Form. *He edited* The Dial
magazine in the 1920s with Marianne Moore, and he set the type for The
Dial's *first printing of T. S. Eliot's "The Waste-Land." His* Collected Poems
1917-1967 *appeared in 1968.*

Poems of Abandonment

(to Libbie, who cleared out)

I. Genius Loci

Until you died, my Love
Somehow I had belief in fear of ghosts.
But now, in this lonely place
that is so full of you
whereby I am not in my essence over-lonesome,

what lovelier
than if your spirit,
the genius of this house,
did materialize right here before me?

Dear Love,
always I tried to earn you,
but now you are the absolutely given

while I each night
lie conscious

of my loss

II. Postlude

When something goes, some other takes its place.
Maybe a thistle where had been a rose;
or where lace was, next time a churchman's missal.
Erase, efface (Life says) when something goes.

Her death leaves such a tangled aftergrowth,
By God I fear I have outlived us both.

The Wrens

The wrens are back!

Their liquid song, pouring across the lawn—
(Or, if the sunlight pours, the wren's song glitters)
Up from the porch,
                    Into the bedroom, where
It is the play of light across a pond,
Sounding as small waves look: new copper coins
Between the seer and the sun.

                    Herewith
Is made a contract binding the brightly waked
Sleeper and his wren, neither the wren's
Nor his, but differently owned by both.

Behind the giving-forth, wren history;
Man-history behind the taking-in.

(Mark the city as a place where no
Wrens sing, as though April were seas of sand,
With spring not the burial of lilac,
                    but heat quaking above stone.)

                    After magnetic storms
Had made all men uneasy, but those the most
That feared the loss of salary or love,

The wrens are back!

JOHN CIARDI

(1916 – 1985)

∞

Lived in Metuchen. He published many volumes of poetry in his lifetime, served in World War II, taught at Harvard and Rutgers, was poetry editor of The Saturday Review, *and made a very popular translation of Dante's* Divine Comedy.

The Catalpa

The catalpa's white week is ending there
in its corner of my yard. It has its arms full
of its own flowering now, but the least air
spins off a petal and a breeze lets fall
whole coronations. There is not much more
of what this is. Is every gladness quick?
That tree's a nuisance, really. Long before
the summer's out, its beans, long as a stick,
will start to shed. And every year one limb
cracks without falling off and hangs there dead
till I get up and risk my neck to trim
what it knows how to lose but not to shed.
I keep it only for this one white pass.
The end of June's its garden; July, its Fall;
all else, the world remembering what it was
in the seven days of its visible miracle.

What should I keep if averages were all?

THEODORE WEISS

(1916 – 2003)

⚭

An award-winning poet. With his wife, Renée, he edited and published
Quarterly Review of Literature *for nearly 60 years. His poems appeared in*
prominent literary magazines and anthologies. His books of poetry include
The Catch *(1951),* Gunsight *(1962),* From Princeton One Autumn
Afternoon: The Collected Poems of Theodore Weiss 1950–1986 *(1987)*
and Selected Poems *(1995).*

The Fire at Alexandria

Imagine it, a Sophocles complete,
the lost epic of Homer, including no doubt
his notes, his journals, and his observations
on blindness. But what occupies me most,
with the greatest hurt of grandeur, are those
magnificent authors, kept in scholarly rows,
whose names we have no passing record of:
scrolls unrolling Aphrodite like Cleopatra
bundled in a rug, the spoils of love.

Crated masterpieces on the wharf,
and never opened, somehow started first.
And then, as though by imitation, the library
took. One book seemed to inspire another,
to remind it of the flame enclosed
within its papyrus like a drowsy torch.
The fire, roused perhaps by what it read,
its reedy song, raged Dionysian, a band
of Corybantes, down the halls now headlong.

The scribes, despite the volumes wept
unable to douse the witty conflagration—
spicy too as Sappho, coiling, melted
with her girls: the Nile no less, reflecting,
burned—saw splendor fled, a day consummate
in twilit ardencies. Troy at its climax
(towers finally topless) could not have been
more awesome, not though the aromatic house
of Priam mortised the passionate moment.

Now whenever I look into a flame,
I try to catch a single countenance:
Cleopatra, winking out from every spark;
Tiresias eye to eye; a magnitude, long lost,
restored to the sky and the stars he once
struck unsuspected parts of into words.
Fire, and I see them resurrected,
madly crackling perfect birds, the world
lit up as by a golden school, the flashings
of the fathoms of set eyes.

RICHARD WILBUR

(b. 1921)

∞

Born in New York, he grew up in an old house in North Caldwell where his family moved when he was two, and where he says he "developed a taste for country things." Named Poet Laureate of the United States in 1987, he has received many honors and awards for his poetry (including two Pulitzer Prizes and a National Book Award). His first book of poems, The Beautiful Changes, *appeared in 1947; his newest book is* Collected Poems 1943–2004. *He now lives and writes in Massachusetts and Key West.*

Jorge Guillén: The Horses

Shaggy and heavily natural, they stand
Immobile under their thick and cumbrous manes,
Pent in a barbed enclosure which contains,
By way of compensation, grazing-land.

Nothing disturbs them now. In slow increase
They fatten like the grass. Doomed to be idle,
To haul no cart or wagon, wear no bridle,
They grow into a vegetable peace.

Soul is the issue of so strict a fate.
They harbor visions in their waking eyes,
And with their quiet ears participate
In heaven's pure serenity, which lies
So near all things—yet from the beasts concealed.
Serene now, superhuman, they crop their field.

Advice to a Prophet

When you come, as you soon must, to the streets of our city,
Mad-eyed from stating the obvious,
Not proclaiming our fall but begging us
In God's name to have self-pity,

Spare us all word of the weapons, their force and range,
The long numbers that rocket the mind;
Our slow, unreckoning hearts will be left behind,
Unable to fear what is too strange.

Nor shall you scare us with talk of the death of the race.
How should we dream of this place without us?—
The sun mere fire, the leaves untroubled about us,
A stone look on the stone's face?

Speak of the world's own change. Though we cannot conceive
Of an undreamt thing, we know to our cost
How the dreamt cloud crumbles, the vines are blackened by frost,
How the view alters. We could believe,

If you told us so, that the white-tailed deer will slip
Into perfect shade, grown perfectly shy,
The lark avoid the reaches of our eye,
The jack-pine lose its knuckled grip

On the cold ledge, and every torrent burn
As Xanthus once, its gliding trout
Stunned in a twinkling. What should we be without
The dolphin's arc, the dove's return,

These things in which we have seen ourselves and spoken?
Ask us, prophet, how we shall call
Our natures forth when that live tongue is all
Dispelled, that glass obscured or broken

In which we have said the rose of our love and the clean
Horse of our courage, in which beheld
The singing locust of the soul unshelled,
And all we mean or wish to mean.

Ask us, ask us whether with the worldless rose
Our hearts shall fail us; come demanding
Whether there shall be lofty or long standing
When the bronze annals of the oak-tree close.

Love Calls Us to the Things of This World

The eyes open to a cry of pulleys,
And spirited from sleep, the astounded soul
Hangs for a moment bodiless and simple
As false dawn.
                        Outside the open window
The morning air is all awash with angels.

Some are in bed-sheets, some are in blouses,
Some are in smocks: but truly there they are.
Now they are rising together in calm swells
Of halcyon feeling, filling whatever they wear
With the deep joy of their impersonal breathing;

Now they are flying in place, conveying
The terrible speed of their omnipresence, moving
And staying like white water; and now of a sudden
They swoon down into so rapt a quiet
That nobody seems to be there.
                        The soul shrinks

From all that it is about to remember,
From the punctual rape of every blessèd day,
And cries,
            "Oh, let there by nothing on earth but laundry,
Nothing but rosy hands in the rising steam
And clear dances done in the sight of heaven."

Yet, as the sun acknowledges
With a warm look the world's hunks and colors,
The soul descends once more in bitter love
To accept the waking body, saying now
In a changed voice as the man yawns and rises,

"Bring them down from their ruddy gallows;
Let there be clean linen for the backs of thieves;
Let lovers go fresh and sweet to be undone,
And the heaviest nuns walk in a pure floating
Of dark habits,
                keeping their difficult balance."

DENISE LEVERTOV

(1923 – 1997)

∞

Taught at Drew University in Madison. Author of many books of poetry and several collections of essays, she served as poetry editor of The Nation *in the early 1960s. Her poems are intellectual and emotional forces of political and moral outrage.*

The Ache of Marriage

The ache of marriage:

thigh and tongue, beloved,
are heavy with it,
it throbs in the teeth

We look for communion
and are turned away, beloved,
each and each

It is leviathan and we
in its belly
looking for joy, some joy
not to be known outside it

two by two in the ark of
the ache of it.

O Taste and See

The world is
not with us enough.
O taste and see

the subway Bible poster said,
meaning **The Lord,** meaning
if anything all that lives
to the imagination's tongue,

grief, mercy, language,
tangerine, weather, to
breathe them, bite,
savor, chew, swallow, transform

into our flesh our
deaths, crossing the street, plum, quince,
living in the orchard and being

hungry, and plucking
the fruit.

Mad Song

My madness is dear to me.
I who was almost always the sanest among my friends,
one to whom others came for comfort,
now at my breasts (that look timid and ignorant,
      that don't look as if milk had flowed from them,
      years gone by)
cherish a viper.
         Hail, little serpent of useless longing
that may destroy me,
that bites me with such idle
needle teeth.

I who am loved by those who love me
for honesty,
to whom life was an honest breath
      taken in good faith,
I've forgotten how to tell joy from bitterness.

Dear to me, dear to me,
blue poison, green pain in the mind's veins.
How am I to be cured against my will?

GERALDINE CLINTON LITTLE

(1925 – 1997)

∽

Her books include Hakugai: Poem From a Concentration Camp *(a book-length narrative poem on the incarceration of Japanese-Americans during* World War II*);* A Well-Tuned Harp; Heloise & Abelard: A Verse Play *(given its premiere performance at The Nicholas Roerich Museum, New York City, in March, 1990).*

Creek Rites

Almost defeated by city heat
we drove there, to swim.
From the grassy treeless bank
we'd push off to the other.
The color of the creek was brown; it was
peaceful, opaque water over-
hung on one side by mazes
of trees we couldn't name, and clotted
brush. We swam through shadows of high
fragrant greenery to where a rope dangled
from a flower-spangled tree, two sisters
free of parenting too proper
for our fancies.

Shinnying up, once, I felt something,
rubbed by bark, between my thighs
explode to a field crazy with sun
and flowers whose petals all were stars
I lay on moaning, mooning.
Almost, almost, I fell away
to only prickly brush before
strangling the branch with frantic love.

Hang on the rope. Hurry. Dazed
with what I didn't know
I grasped the thick tickling coil
my sister began to swing, bells
in my head donging dizzy changes,
at last, over the receptive water,
dropped through air heavy with summer
stillness, into my shadow floating
among lilies one dragonfly iridesced.

Still I recall how there was nothing
behind the shape I fractured, nothing
but cold and clutching roots. Then
I popped into my bones, flesh
like a secret found
in moist, mysterious depths.

GERALD STERN

(b. 1925)

∽

Author of nine collections of poetry, has won many awards, most recently the Ruth Lilly Poetry Prize. Other awards include a fellowship from the Academy of American Poets and The Lamont Poetry Prize.

The Dancing

In all these rotten shops, in all this broken furniture
and wrinkled ties and baseball trophies and coffee pots
I have never seen a postwar Philco
with the automatic eye
nor heard Ravel's "Bolero" the way I did
in 1945 in that tiny living room
on Beechwood Boulevard, nor danced as I did
then, my knives all flashing, my hair all streaming,
my mother red with laughter, my father cupping
his left hand under his armpit, doing the dance
of old Ukraine, the sound of his skin half drum,
half fart, the world at last a meadow,
the three of us whirling and singing, the three of us
screaming and falling, as if we were dying,
as if we could never stop—in 1945—
in Pittsburgh, beautiful filthy Pittsburgh, home
of the evil Mellons, 5,000 miles away
from the other dancing—in Poland and Germany—
oh God of mercy, oh wild God.

Lucky Life

Lucky life isn't one long string of horrors
and there are moments of peace, and pleasure, as I lie in between
    the blows.
Lucky I don't have to wake up in Phillipsburg, New Jersey,
on the hill overlooking Union Square or the hill overlooking
Kuebler Brewery or the hill overlooking SS. Philip and James
but have my own hills and my own vistas to come back to.

Each year I go down to the island I add
one more year to the darkness;
and though I sit up with my dear friends
trying to separate the one year from the other,
this one from the last, that one from the former,
another from another,
after a while they all get lumped together,
the year we walked to Holgate,
the year our shoes got washed away,
the year it rained,
the year my tooth brought misery to us all.

This year was a crisis. I knew it when we pulled
the car onto the sand and looked for the key.
I knew it when we walked up the outside steps
and opened the hot icebox and began the struggle
with swollen drawers and I knew it when we laid out
the sheets and separated the clothes into piles
and I knew it when we made our first rush onto
the beach and I knew it when we finally sat
on the porch with coffee cups shaking in our hands.

My dream is I'm walking through Phillipsburg, New Jersey,
and I'm lost on South Main Street. I am trying to tell,
by memory, which statue of Christopher Columbus
I have to look for, the one with him slumped over
and lost in weariness or the one with him
vaguely guiding the way with a cross and globe in
one hand and a compass in the other.
My dream is I'm in the Eagle Hotel on Chamber Street
sitting at the oak bar, listening to two
obese veterans discussing Hawaii in 1942,
and reading the funny signs over the bottles.
My dream is I sleep upstairs over the honey locust
and sit on the side porch overlooking the stone culvert
with a whole new set of friends, mostly old and humorless.

Dear waves, what will you do for me this year?
Will you drown out my scream?
Will you let me rise through the fog?
Will you fill me with that old salt feeling?
Will you let me take my long steps in the cold sand?
Will you let me lie on the white bedspread and study
the black clouds with the blue holes in them?
Will you let me see the rusty trees and the old monoplanes
      one more year?
Will you still let me draw my sacred figures
and move the kites and the birds around with my dark mind?

Lucky life is like this. Lucky there is an ocean to come to.
Lucky you can judge yourself in this water.
Lucky you can be purified over and over again.
Lucky there is the same cleanliness for everyone.
Lucky life is like that. Lucky life. Oh lucky life.
Oh lucky lucky life. Lucky life.

On The Island

After cheating each other for eighteen years
this husband and this wife are trying to do something with the three
days they still have left before they go back to the city;
and after cheating the world for fifty years these two old men
touch the rosy skin under their white hair and try to remember
the days of solid brass and real wood
before the Jews came onto the island.
They are worried about the trees in India
and the corruption in the Boy Scouts
and the climbing interest rate,
but most of all they spend their time remembering
the beach the way it was in the early thirties
when all the big hotels here were shaped like Greek churches.

Me, I think about salt
and how my life will one day be clean and simple
if only I can reduce it all to salt,
how I will no longer lie down like a tired dog,
whispering and sighing before I go to sleep,
how I will be able to talk to someone
without going from pure joy to silence
and touch someone
without going from truth to concealment.

Salt is the only thing that lasts on this island.
It gets into the hair, into the eyes, into the clothes,
into the wood, into the metal.
Everything is going to disappear here but the salt.
The flags will go, the piers,
the gift shops, the golf courses, the clam bars,
and the telephone poles and the rows of houses and the string of cars.

I like to think of myself turned to salt
and all that I love turned to salt;
I like to think of coating whatever is left
with my own tongue and fingers.
I like to think of floating again in my first home,
still remembering the warm rock
and its slow destruction,
still remembering the first conversion to blood
and the forcing of the sea into those cramped vessels.

MAXINE KUMIN

(b. 1925)

⌒⌒

*Born in Philadelphia, she spent summers with her family in Atlantic City.
Her eleven books of poems include the 1972 Pulitzer Prize winner,* Up
Country: Poems of New England. *A former Consultant in Poetry to the
Library of Congress, she has been Poet Laureate of New Hampshire where
she lives.*

How It Goes On

Today I trade my last unwise
ewe lamb, the one who won't leave home,
for two cords of stove-length oak
and wait on the old enclosed
front porch to make the swap.
November sun revives the thick
trapped buzz of horseflies. The siren
for noon and forest fires blows
a sliding scale. The lamb of woe
looks in at me through glass
on the last day of her life.

Geranium scraps from the window box
trail from her mouth, burdock burrs
are stickered to her fleece like chicken pox,
under her tail stub, permanent smears.

I think of how it goes on,
this dark particular bent of our hungers:
the way wire eats into a tree
year after year on the pasture's perimeter,
keeping the milk cows penned
until they grow too old to freshen;
of how the last wild horses were scoured
from canyons in Idaho, roped, thrown,
their nostrils twisted shut with wire
to keep them down, the mares aborting,
days later, all of them carted to town.

I think of how it will be
in January, nights so cold
the pond ice cracks like target practice,
daylight glue-colored, sleet falling,
my yellow horse slick with the ball-bearing
sleet, raising up from his dingy browse
out of boredom and habit
to strip bark from the fenced-in trees;
of February, month of the hard palate,
the split wood running out,
worms working in the flour bin.

The lamb, whose time has come, goes off
in the cab of the dump truck, tied to the seat
with baling twine, durable enough
to bear her to the knife and rafter.

O lambs! The whole wolf-world sits down to eat
and cleans its muzzle after.

A. R. AMMONS

(1926 – 2001)

∞

Lived for a decade in southern coastal New Jersey working at a glass factory before beginning a teaching career at Cornell in 1964. Here he wrote "Gravelly Run," one of his transcendental epiphanies, which manifests his perception of the interrelatedness of all that is ("for it is not so much to know the self / as to know it as it is known / by galaxy and cedar cone").

Gravelly Run

I don't know somehow it seems sufficient
to see and hear whatever coming and going is,
losing the self to the victory
       of stones and trees,
of bending sandpit lakes, crescent
round groves of dwarf pine:

for it is not so much to know the self
as to know it as it is known
       by galaxy and cedar cone,
as if birth had never found it
and death could never end it:

the swamp's slow water comes
down Gravelly Run fanning the long
    stone-held algal
hair and narrowing roils between
the shoulders of the highway bridge:

holly grows on the banks in the woods there,
and the cedar's gothic-clustered
    spires could make
green religion in winter bones:

so I look and reflect, but the air's glass
jail seals each thing in its entity:

no use to make any philosophies here:
    I see no
god in the holly, hear no song from
the snowbroken weeds: Hegel is not the winter
yellow in the pines: the sunlight has never
heard of trees: surrendered self among
    unwelcoming forms: stranger,
hoist your burdens, get on down the road.

Motion Which Disestablishes
Organizes Everything

William James (*The Varieties of Religious Experience,* p. 84)
    is to be
commended for penning out of our finest recommendations
    for the bright outlook:

he was so miserable himself he knew how to put a fine point
    on the exact
prescription: he knew that anybody who knows anything
    about human

existence knows it can be heavy; in fact, it can be so heavy
    it can undo
its own heaviness, the knees can crumple, the breath
    and heart beat,

not to mention the bowels, can become irregular, etc.:
    but the world,
William knew, sardonic and skeptical, can characterize
    sufferers of such

symptoms malingering wimps, a heaviness not to be welcomed
    by a person who
like me feels like one of those: weight begets weight and
    nature works as well

(and mindlessly) down as up; you have to put english
    of your own into
the act misleading the way into lightenings: brightness,
    however

desirable, is a losing battle, though, and James knew it can be
    depended on
more often than not that folks won't have spare brightness
    on them every

morning that they want your heaviness to cost them:
    so, in general, if
someone asks how you are, no matter how you are, say
    something nice: say,

"fine," or "marvelous morning," and, this way, hell gradually
    notches up
toward paradise, a misconstruction many conspire to forward
    because

nearly all, maybe all, prefer one to the other: oppositions
    make things costly:
crooked teeth encourage the symmetry of braces but as soon
    as everybody's

teeth are perfect, crooked teeth misalign: something is
    always working
the other way: if you let the other way go, you get more in
    Dutch for

while the other way at first may constitute an alternative
    mainstream,
pretty soon it breaks up into dispersive tributaries and
    splinters a

rondure of fine points into branches and brooklets
    till it becomes
impossible to get a hold on it, a river system running
    backwards:

be bright: that is a wish that can be stable: you can always
    think of
happiness because it's wished right out of any rubbings
    with reality, so

you can keep the picture pure and steady: I always imagine
    a hillock,
about as much as I can get up these days, with a lovely
    shade tree and under

the tree this beautiful girl, unnervingly young, who
    projects golden
worlds: this scene attracts me so much that even though
    I'm a little

scared by it it feels enlivening, a rosy, sweet enlivening:
    poets
can always prevent our hubris, reminding us how the
    coffin slats peel

cloth and crack in, how the onset of time strikes at birth, how
    love falters
how past the past is, how the eyes of hungry children feed
    the flies.

ALLEN GINSBERG

(1926 – 1997)

∞

*Born in Newark and raised in Paterson, attended Columbia University
before gaining recognition as the key poetic figure in the literary revolution
known as "the Beat Generation." William Carlos Williams wrote the intro-
duction for his* Howl; Kaddish, *perhaps his greatest poem, is an elegy for
his mother, Naomi. As an antiwar activist and counter culture prophet, his
influence on younger generations worldwide remains enormous.*

A Supermarket in California

What thoughts I have of you tonight, Walt Whitman, for I walked
down the sidestreets under the trees with a headache self-conscious
looking at the full moon.

In my hungry fatigue, and shopping for images, I went into the
neon fruit supermarket, dreaming of your enumerations!

What peaches and what penumbras! Whole families shopping at
night! Aisles full of husbands! Wives in the avocados, babies in the
tomatoes!—and you, García Lorca, what were you doing down by
the watermelons?

I saw you, Walt Whitman, childless, lonely old grubber, poking
among the meats in the refrigerator and eyeing the grocery boys.

I heard you asking questions of each: Who killed the pork chops?
What price bananas? Are you my Angel?

I wandered in and out of the brilliant stacks of cans following
you, and followed in my imagination by the store detective.

We strode down the open corridors together in our solitary fancy
tasting artichokes, possessing every frozen delicacy, and never
passing the cashier.

Where are we going, Walt Whitman? The doors close in an hour.
Which way does your beard point tonight?

(I touch your book and dream of our odyssey in the supermarket
and feel absurd.)

Will we walk all night through solitary streets? The trees add
shade to shade, lights out in the houses, we'll both be lonely.

Will we stroll dreaming of the lost America of love past blue
automobiles in driveways, home to our silent cottage?

Ah, dear father, graybeard, lonely old courage-teacher, what
America did you have when Charon quit poling his ferry and you got
out on a smoking bank and stood watching the boat disappear on
the black waters of Lethe?

To Aunt Rose

Aunt Rose—now—might I see you
with your thin face and buck tooth smile and pain
        of rheumatism—and a long black heavy shoe
           for your bony left leg
limping down the long hall in Newark on the running carpet
    past the black grand piano
        in the day room
           where the parties were
        and I sang Spanish loyalist songs
          in a high squeaky voice
              (hysterical) the committee listening
          while you limped around the room
          collected the money—
Aunt Honey, Uncle Sam, a stranger with a cloth arm
    in his pocket
        and huge young bald head
           of Abraham Lincoln Brigade

—your long sad face
    your tears of sexual frustration
        (what smothered sobs and bony hips
          under the pillows of Osborne Terrace)
—the time I stood on the toilet seat naked
    and you powdered my thighs with calamine
        against the poison ivy—my tender
          and shamed first black curled hairs
what were you thinking in secret heart then
        knowing me a man already—
and I an ignorant girl of family silence on the thin pedestal
        of my legs in the bathroom—Museum of Newark.

                    Aunt Rose
Hitler is dead, Hitler is in Eternity; Hitler is with
              Tamburlane and Emily Brontë
Though I see you walking still, a ghost on Osborne Terrace
              down the long dark hall to the front door
          limping a little with a pinched smile
          in what must have been a silken
                    flower dress
    welcoming my father, the Poet, on his visit to Newark
          —see you arriving in the living room
              dancing on your crippled leg
          and clapping hands his book
              had been accepted by Liveright

Hitler is dead and Liveright's gone out of business
The Attic of the Past and *Everlasting Minute* are out of print
              Uncle Harry sold his last silk stocking
      Claire quit interpretive dancing school
                  Buba sits a wrinkled monument in Old
                  Ladies Home blinking at new babies

last time I saw you was the hospital
      pale skull protruding under ashen skin
          blue veined unconscious girl
              in an oxygen tent
      the war in Spain has ended long ago
              Aunt Rose

W. S. MERWIN

(b. 1927)

∽

Born in Union City, educated at Princeton, he has written fifteen award-winning books of poetry, including The Carrier of Ladders, *which won the 1970 Pulitzer Prize. He writes on his farm in Hawaii, which he devotes to the environmental preservation of the Hawaiian Islands. Copper Canyon published* Migration: New and Selected Poems *and his sixteenth volume of poetry,* Present Company, *in 2005.*

Leviathan

This is the black sea-brute bulling through wave-wrack,
Ancient as ocean's shifting hills, who in sea-toils
Travelling, who furrowing the salt acres
Heavily, his wake hoary behind him,
Shoulders spouting, the fist of his forehead
Over wastes gray-green crashing, among horses unbroken
From bellowing fields, past bone-wreck of vessels,
Tide-ruin, wash of lost bodies bobbing
No longer sought for, and islands of ice gleaming,
Who ravening the rank flood, wave-marshalling,
Overmastering the dark sea-marches, finds home
And harvest. Frightening to foolhardiest
Mariners, his size were difficult to describe:
The hulk of him is like hills heaving,
Dark, yet as crags of drift-ice, crowns cracking in thunder,
Like land's self by night black-looming, surf churning and trailing
Along his shores' rushing, shoal-water boding
About the dark of his jaws; and who should moor at his edge
And fare on afoot would find gates of no gardens,

But the hill of dark underfoot diving,
Closing overhead, the cold deep, and drowning.
He is called Leviathan, and named for rolling,
First created he was of all creatures,
He has held Jonah three days and nights,
He is that curling serpent that in ocean is,
Sea-fright he is, and the shadow under the earth.
Days there are, nonetheless, when he lies
Like an angel, although a lost angel
On the waste's unease, no eye of man moving,
Bird hovering, fish flashing, creature whatever
Who after him came to herit earth's emptiness.
Froth at flanks seething soothes to stillness,
Waits; with one eye he watches
Dark of night sinking last, with one eye dayrise
As at first over foaming pastures. He makes no cry
Though that light is a breath. The sea curling,
Star-climbed, wind-combed, cumbered with itself still
As at first it was, is the hand not yet contented
Of the Creator. And he waits for the world to begin.

The Drunk in the Furnace

For a good decade
The furnace stood in the naked gully, fireless
And vacant as any hat. Then when it was
No more to them than a hulking black fossil
To erode unnoticed with the rest of the junk-hill
By the poisonous creek, and rapidly to be added
  To their ignorance,

  They were afterwards astonished
To confirm, one morning, a twist of smoke like a pale
Resurrection, staggering out of its chewed hole,
And to remark then other tokens that someone,
Cosily bolted behind the eye-holed iron
Door of the drafty burner, had there established
  His bad castle.

  Where he gets his spirits
It's a mystery. But the stuff keeps him musical:
Hammer-and-anvilling with poker and bottle
To his jugged bellowings, till the last groaning clang
As he collapses onto the rioting
Springs of a litter of car-seats ranged on the grates,
  To sleep like an iron pig.

  In their tar-paper church
On a text about stoke-holes that are sated never
Their Reverend lingers. They nod and hate trespassers.
When the furnace wakes, though, all afternoon
Their witless offspring flock like piped rats to its siren
Crescendo, and agape on the crumbling ridge
  Stand in a row and learn.

Fog-Horn

Surely that moan is not the thing
That men thought they were making, when they
Put it there, for their own necessities.
That throat does not call to anything human
But to something men had forgotten,
That stirs under fog. Who wounded that beast
Incurably, or from whose pasture
Was it lost, full grown, and time closed round it
With no way back? Who tethered its tongue
So that its voice could never come
To speak out in the light of clear day,
But only when the shifting blindness
Descends and is acknowledged among us,
As though from under a floor it is heard,
Or as though from behind a wall, always
Nearer than we had remembered? If it
Was we that gave tongue to this cry
What does it bespeak in us, repeating
And repeating, insisting on something
That we never meant? We only put it there
To give warning of something we dare not
Ignore, lest we should come upon it
Too suddenly, recognize it too late,
As our cries were swallowed up and all hands lost.

JEAN HOLLANDER

(b. 1928)

∞

A professor of creative writing at several colleges and universities and director of the annual Writers Conference at The College of New Jersey, she is author of several books of poetry, including Crushed into Honey, *and co-author (with her husband, Robert) of a highly praised translation of Dante's* Divine Comedy.

End of Memory

What can I bring you
after ten long years?
If you had lived
you would have been
too old for tears.
I pluck a sprig of purple flowering
that dried all winter and I set
it broken in the crust of snow
where deer have hoofed
embroidery of nightly visiting
around your stone.
From horror that remains
I raise you tall as I
your otherness, blue eyes, blond hair,
against my dark, having forgotten all
the details of your face except
your head against my neck
and that my last consoling was
to wash your things as though
you still could wear.

X. J. KENNEDY

(b. 1929)

∽

A native of Dover, New Jersey, he has published seven collections of poetry (including The Lords of Misrule *(2002),* Nude Descending a Staircase *(1961),* Cross Ties *(1985), and* Dark Horses *(1992), 18 children's books, and several textbooks, including* An Introduction to Poetry *with Dana Gioia, now in its eleventh edition. His honors include the 2004 Poets Prize and the Shelley Memorial Award.*

In a Prominent Bar in Secaucus One Day

To the tune of "The Old Orange Flute"
or the tune of "Sweet Betsy from Pike"

In a prominent bar in Secaucus one day
Rose a lady in skunk with a topheavy sway,
Raised a knobby red finger—all turned from their beer—
While with eyes bright as snowcrust she sang high and clear:

"Now who of you'd think from an eyeload of me
That I once was a lady as proud as could be?
Oh I'd never sit down by a tumbledown drunk
If it wasn't, my dears, for the high cost of junk.

"All the gents used to swear that the white of my calf
Beat the down of the swan by a length and a half.
In the kerchief of linen I caught to my nose
Ah, there never fell snot, but a little gold rose.

"I had seven gold teeth and a toothpick of gold,
My Virginia cheroot was a leaf of it rolled
And I'd light it each time with a thousand in cash—
Why the bums used to fight if I flicked them an ash.

"Once the toast of the Biltmore, the belle of the Taft,
I would drink bottle beer at the Drake, never draft,
And dine at the Astor on Salisbury steak
With a clean tablecloth for each bite I did take.

"In a car like the Roxy I'd roll to the track,
A steel-guitar trio, a bar in the back,
And the wheels made no noise, they turned over so fast,
Still it took you ten minutes to see me go past.

"When the horses bowed down to me that I might choose,
I bet on them all, for I hated to lose.
Now I'm saddled each night for my butter and eggs
And the broken threads race down the backs of my legs.

"Let you hold in mind, girls, that your beauty must pass
Like a lovely white clover that rusts with its grass.
Keep your bottoms off barstools and marry you young
Or be left—an old barrel with many a bung.

"For when time takes you out for a spin in his car
You'll be hard-pressed to stop him from going too far
And be left by the roadside, for all your good deeds,
Two toadstools for tits and a face full of weeds."

All the house raised a cheer, but the man at the bar
Made a phonecall and up pulled a red patrol car
And she blew us a kiss as they copped her away
From that prominent bar in Secaucus, N.J.

Five-and-Dime, Late Thirties

Your nose by frying franks'
    Salt pungent odor stung,
You'd perch a stool, give thanks
    For shreds of turkey strung

On a mound of stuffing doled
    With icecream scoop, lone spoon
Of gray canned peas, one cold
    Roll, cranberry half-moon.

The same recorded air
    Swung round the counters daily:
Once more, "Old Rocking Chair"
    Recaptured Mildred Bailey.

Inclined, some lone gray head
    Off in a dream apart,
Selecting glasses, read
    With slow lips from a chart.

Nearby, a rouge-cheeked jade
    In permanent spit curls
Pushed Maybelline eyeshade
    To adolescent girls.

At times a beaten bell
    Insistent as Big Ben
Proclaimed the news: some swell
    Had tried to change a ten.

On to the thick cheap pads,
    Your last saved dime to blow,
To write fresh Iliads
    You'd steer course, even though

You longed for chocolates
    From the open-air glass case
Where, nightly, hordes of rats
    Shat in the licorice lace

Until one day the Board
    Of Health padlocked the door.
As sure as FDR
    Had kept us out of war,

Brown Shirts were just a show,
    Hitler a comic wraith
Far off. What you don't know
    Won't hurt had been our faith.

For Allen Ginsberg

Ginsberg, Ginsberg, burning bright,
Taunter of the ultra right,
What blink of the Buddha's eye
Chose the day for you to die?

Queer pied piper, howling wild,
Mantra-minded flower child,
Queen of Maytime, misrule's lord,
Bawling, *Drop out! All aboard!*

Foe of fascist, bane of bomb,
Finger-cymbaled, chanting OM,
Proper poets' thorn-in-side,
Turner of a whole time's tide,

Who can fill your sloppy shoes?
What a catch for Death. We lose
Glee and sweetness, freaky light,
Ginsberg, Ginsberg, burning bright.

GLORIA ROVDER HEALY

(b. 1933)

∞

Born in Monmouth County, poet consultant to the Long Branch Poetry
Festival, she is editor of the poetry anthology of the shore region entitled
Poetic Reflections of Monmouth County *(Northwind, 2004).*

The Power and the Glory

On the first day of school,
after we recited the Our Father.
You came to my desk,
pressed the rubber tip of your crutch
on my chest, told me to stand,
repeat the prayer for the class.

I knotted the hem of my skirt as I
tried to pronounce each word correctly.
Did she forget anything, children?
Billy Slezak jumped out of his seat and
recited words I'd never heard . . .
For thine is the kingdom and the power
and the glory. Ahmen

I didn't forget, Miss Norman
I don't say it that way.
We say it that way, don't we Billy?
And we don't have to go to Sunday school
to learn to say Ahmen, do we?
Did you hear her say Aymen?
Billy snickered, Yes, Miss Norman.

I hated Billy—he could recite times tables
from memory, spell words like toilet backwards.
After school, he'd wash blackboards, clap erasers
or put a new rubber tip on your crutch.

At Christmas, you took the class to your house
to see your aquariums, your tropical fish
You looked like the pope sitting in your red
Velvet chair with the class at your feet—except Billy.
His chair was in front of the aquarium.

Don't let Gloria near my fish, Billy.
She always eats fish on Friday.

I didn't eat your fish and I didn't eat
the sweet sugar cookies you served either.
I wrapped them in a red linen napkin
took them home and put them
in my dresser drawer with a sweater
that didn't fit anymore.

When the cookies turned to crumbs
I threw them in the garbage but
saved the fancy linen napkin.

Years later, my house burned down
and your napkin, with the letter
"N" embroidered in one corner,
went up in smoke.

Yet, no matter how hard I try to slam the door
on you and Billy Slezak you pry it open
with that hard rubber tip on the end
of your menacing crutch.

AMIRI BARAKA

(b. 1934)

∞

Born Everett LeRoi Jones in Newark, he is poet, author, playwright, Marxist African-American political activist, director, and publisher. In 2002 he was named New Jersey's second Poet Laureate, a position abolished by the New Jersey legislature after his incendiary poem, "Somebody Blew Up America," considered anti-Semitic, ignited a major national protest.

Monk's World

'Round Midnight

That street where midnight
is round, the moon flat
& blue, where fire engines solo
& cats stand around & look
is Monk's world

When I last saw him, turning around
high from 78 RPM, growling
a landscape of spaced funk

When I last spoke to him, coming out
the Vanguard, he hipped me to
my own secrets, like Nat
he dug the numbers & letters
blowing through the grass
initials & invocations of the past

All the questions I asked Monk He
       answered first
       in a beret. Why was
       a high priest staring
       Why were the black keys
       signifying. And who was
       wrapped in common magic
       like a street empty of everything
       except weird birds

The last time Monk smiled I read
       the piano's diary. His fingers
       where he collected yr feelings
       The Bar he circled to underscore
       the anonymous laughter of smoke
       & posters.

Monk carried equations he danced at you.
       "What's happening?" We said, as he dipped &
       spun. "What's happening?"

"Everything. All the time.
       Everything googoplex
       of a second."

Like a door, he opened, not disappearing
       but remaining a distant profile
       of intimate revelation.

Oh, man! Monk was digging Trane now
       w/o a chaser he drank himself
       in. & Trane reported from
       the 6th or 7th planet deep in

       the Theloniuscape.

Where fire engines screamed the blues
    & night had a shiny mouth
    & scatted flying things.

Preface to a Twenty Volume Suicide Note
For Kellie Jones, born 16 May 1959

Lately, I've become accustomed to the way
The ground opens up and envelopes me
Each time I go out to walk the dog.
Or the broad edged silly music the wind
Makes when I run for a bus . . .

Things have come to that.

And now, each night I count the stars,
And each night I get the same number.
And when they will not come to be counted,
I count the holes they leave.

Nobody sings anymore.

And then last night, I tiptoed up
To my daughter's room and heard her
Talking to someone, and when I opened
The door, there was no one there . . .
Only she on her knees, peeking into

Her own clasped hands.

MADELINE TIGER
(b. 1934)

❧

Teaches in the "Writers in the Schools" Program of the New Jersey State Council on the Arts. Most recent of her eight collections are My Father's Harmonica, Mary of Migdal, White Owl, *and the "new and selected"* Birds of Sorrow and Joy *(Marsh Hawk Press, 2003).*

Learning to Read *Sky*
for *Wai Gong* and *Wai Pó*

Solstice gone, the New Year
parades its dragons down town
No sign from the ancient sky or
from any writings could have predicted
the mingling of our blood
which has brought you to this towering city
where I was born

or that you would teach me
the characters for *water, fire, sky, sun, moon,*
star, flower, grass, mountain, big brother, little brother
and the verbs for *eat* and for *like,*
which means something more like *treasure*

and for *writing* and *study,*
making lists that I find
even in the new year sweeter
than the Tseu Ye songs
might have been

I don't complain of being too old
to make offerings
like the "singing girls"
or to expect orchids for my little boat

When you, Pó, held
the little one, two years heavy,
pacing until he fell asleep
and Gong brewed green tea, I thought
of the great safety, and I felt
joy over that weight in your slim arms

I looked lightly at your bent back and
thought of time—how you have contained it
and made it slow down like an obedient transport
I thought of the two boys at peace, their beautiful
eyelashes. I noticed the construction noises

twenty-seven flights below, outside, and it was still
calm here, as the character for *home,* as the untroubled
sky. I thought of what you taught me about the characters
for *yesterday, today,* and *tomorrow,* how they are all built
on the character for *sky.* And I let my eyes go
from deep into my tea

to you, at rest with the sleeping boy now,
to the great sky out there, through our large windows,
extending endlessly—west, over the Hudson River,
over this continent, and arching eastward
over the bridges and Narrows and harbors
and the bay and over the dark ocean. I watched
the bright sky slowly going over the world.

Bird Song

My mother is lonely
she is like a lost finch:
she is pecking around her kitchen

My mother is shrinking, shriveled
like a weathered pear,
she is sere

My mother is hanging on:
every little wind moves her,
the world is turbulent

around my mother
She is smaller than
the tall queen with blond curls

who dried me with a huge towel
and tucked me in with trade-wind lullabyes.
My mother is without a song

She watches the news like a hungry
reporter, taking her scotch & water
her Ritz & La Vâche Qui Rit

She goes to bed early
and sleeps like an old fawn
I think she doesn't dare to tremble

Mother's eyes are still as blue
as a placid lake, but clouded
over: nothing crosses her view

She stares flat as a Magritte eye
into the infant sadness
of everything she forgets

Mother is so alone inside
she is startled whenever
I come near her. Poor Mother,

do not be an orphan,
be safe in your warm house,
be cozy with your little dinner

I will come as a bird
and sing
in your window

ROBERT BENSE

(b. 1935)

∞

Raised in southern Illinois, and through work has ended up in the East, living in Lawrenceville and New Brunswick. He teaches English at the local community college in Bucks County, Pennsylvania. His poetry has appeared in Chelsea, Gulf Coast, Poetry, Poetry Northwest, Southern Poetry Review *and* Southern Humanities Review, *among others.*

Halflife of the Finite

Carpenter bees
each summer, precisely
voiding with tap and drill,
riddle bargeboard and porch
frame like carpenters
undoing. After work, go
home, let us alone.

A cricket and kin
find the house in our sleep,
sing their deadman's office
for all larval children—unborn,
unbearable, or borne off like
their own dead in a late
night-scurry.

Yellow jackets
move into the guestroom,
pack food and progeny
into the ceiling, fight hard
to stay, leaking honey.
They leave the rest to us,
risking more than we would.

Arthropods
in procession, chewing,
ingest the world, heralds
of the infinite. Announcing
to whoever will look or listen
behold
the presence of God.

BOB MCKENTY

(b. 1935)

∞

Bob McKenty's poems have appeared in The New York Times, Reader's Digest, *anthologies and textbooks. He loves to do recitations, especially his annual gig at the National Baseball Hall of Fame. He has lived in New Jersey since 1963.*

First Fruit

It was Eden's fine fig tree in bloom
That provided the first bride and groom
    With the underwear which
    Earned the fig its true niche
As original Fruit of the Loom.

The Lamb

He gambols to the shearer's shear
And soon his woolies disappear
And thus he gets his just deserts
For gambolers always lose their shirts.

The Lion

The lethargic lion loafs all day,
On occasion taking paws to prey.

Mystery

The Big Bang blew. From nearly nil
We've grown to this galactic place,
The universe expanding still.
Why can't I find a parking space?

Uneasy Lies the Tooth That Needs a Crown

Uneasy lies the tooth that needs a crown
Requiring first a root canal. Oh, dear!
It next must have its gumline whittled down
By yet another oral engineer.
Ground down by the inexorable drill,
Inured by anesthesia to the ache,
Its lifeblood drained, the Adversary still
Will drive into its heart a metal stake
To which to fix a gold sarcophagus
Entombing one who died (alas!) too young—
Denied fresh air that's lavished upon us
And tender ministrations of the tongue.
    Then, when their fellow tooth's ordeal is done,
    Uneasy lie the other 31.

D. E. STEWARD
(b. 1936)

∞

D. E. Steward's contribution is part of a month in a sequential project that runs month- to- month, under way since September 1986. He was born in April, 1936, across the river from Stockton, New Jersey. One hundred twenty of his months are published in various literary magazines.

Octubre

Awake over the Pacific not far south of Lima

Puddle bays in an ocean-gaping coastline verging into night smog haze out the portside window

Colorless blue-gray soft stardust brilliant

The bulk mass wall of the moonlit Andes behind

All to the horizon on megascale, as if gazing out from low planetary orbit

Moonlight on the water projects colossal reflective plates laid out beside the cusped bays' margins and headlands

Predawn course south-by-southeast into the Southern Cone

Short-day chilly October to long-day far-south early October spring

Already there, well below the equator

And still hours out from Santiago de Chile

Great Andean city lying exactly on the meridian of Martha's Vineyard

At the antipodean latitude of Augusta, Georgia

América

The reaches of our stupendous world

The detail of the headland to headland scape, rock above the surf to rock to hidden inlet

Up and down both ocean coasts of the two long American continents

Urban drift smoke fingers in the moonlight reaching out to sea now from Lima, immense gray dust rainless coastal winter foggy Peruvian megalopolis

Lima at more than seven million, close upon the coast, suspiring predawn cooking-fire smoke as from African bush towns but on a metropolitan scale

Sheet-plastic, zinc corrugated, city-gray dust sprawl reaching across the nearly rainless littoral toward the great city's port of Callao

In the sprawling poverty of the crowded urban world squeezed to the profoundly squalid by the oblivious insouciance of its elites

Five gigantic cities of over ten million in 1975, fourteen in 1995, twenty in 2000

There will be twenty-seven in 2015

Lima, Buenos Aires, Mexico, Los Angeles, Rio, São Paulo-Santos, Bogotá, New York are the big ones so far in the Americas

Newly arrived among them, Santiago, six and a half million plus

It grew by two million in the nineties, has serious inversion layer smog

It lies at about 34° S, like Sydney and Cape Town

Without Cape Town's persistent wind, that so eerily enhances the brilliance of Cape Town's ultimacy

Cape Town's visual weather flow is like fog moving quietly into San Francisco, but more vivid, with much clearer demarcations between cloud and sun

In brilliant sun clouds pour off Table Mountain like liquid air

The city spread below

The Foreshore lifts into the hill streets of old District Six

Cape Town tattooed on the memorial sensorium, cheek on plexiglass staring out in the predawn here and now

She spoke for the first time of his death a few days ago

How in mid-September, early Friday morning, after spending the night lying together talking, he asked her to call his doctor, that he needed to go to the hospital again

He died there before noon

He would have liked to hear about Santiago and beyond

When we talked next time, he would have kicked back in his chair

With each of his gleeful rhonchal snorts he would have tossed off
polished comments about Allende, wine, raising fruit in a
Southern Hemisphere California, copper, ozone holes, fisheries,
Patagonia, Pinochet

He scorned British perfidy and all hypocrisy, his world was
Switzerland, his sons, molecular biology, Rhone Valley three-star
restaurants, California and Tennessee

Charlie, poor Charlie is no more

Skin dry, cabin dry, mouth dry after all night in the lower stratosphere

Slipping away from the coast to cross South America's western bight,
the moonlight and smoke haze blurs the littoral's lines and limits

Over the easternmost reaches of the daunting Pacific

Course line from Panama laid to avoid flight over the high Andes of
Peru and Ecuador, veer off the coast to slant inland only later,
south of the Atacama

Pass roughly over La Serena and Coquimbo

La Serena is close to Vicuña, Gabriela Mistral's papaya-avocado
mountain town

Gabriela Mistral on her way upcountry from Serena toward her sierra
querencia in the rumble seat of a Model A

And sometimes she'd take the train up her valley to Vicuña from the coast

Don't know how she traveled south to Santiago

Possibly by ship, La Serena to Valparaìso

She died in New York . . . .

C. K. WILLIAMS

(b. 1936)

෨

The 2000 Pulitzer-Prize-winning poet spends half the year at Princeton University where he teaches and the other half in France where he lives as a writer. He recently won the National Book Award for Singing.

Invisible Mending

Three women old as angels,
bent as ancient apple trees,
who, in a storefront window,
with magnifying glasses,
needles fine as hair, and shining
scissors, parted woof from warp
and pruned what would in
human tissue have been sick.

Abrasions, rents and frays,
slits and chars and acid
splashes, filaments that gave
way of their own accord
from the stress of spanning
tiny, trifling gaps, but which
in a wounded psyche
make a murderous maze.

Their hands as hard as horn,
their eyes as keen as steel,
the threads they worked with
must have seemed as thick
as ropes on ships, as cables
on a crane, but still their heads
would lower, their teeth bare
to nip away the raveled ends.

Only sometimes would they
lift their eyes to yours to show
how much lovelier than these twists
of silk and serge the garments
of the mind are, yet how much
more benign their implements
than mind's procedures
of forgiveness and repair.

And in your loneliness you'd notice
how really very gently they'd take
the fabric to its last, with what
solicitude gather up worn edges
to be bound, with what severe
but kind detachment wield
their amputating shears:
forgiveness, and repair.

Night

1.

Somehow a light plane
coming in low at three
in the morning to a local airstrip
hits a complex of tones
in its growl so I hear mingled
with it a peal of church bells,
swelling in and out
of audibility, arrhythmic,
but rich and insistent, then,
though I try to hold them,
they dissolve, fade away;
only that monochrome
drone bores on
alone through the dark.

2.

This is one of our new
winters, dry, windless,
and warm, when even
the lightest cover is stifling.
A luxuriant flowering
pear tree used to shelter
the front of our house,
but last August a storm
took it, a bizarrely focused
miniature tornado never
before seen in this climate,
and now the sky outside
the window is raw, the inert
air viscous and sour.

3.

I was ill, and by the merest
chance happened to be
watching as the tree fell.
I saw the branches helplessly
flail, the fork of the trunk
with a great creak split,
and the heavier half start
down, catch on wires,
and hang, lifting and subsiding
in the last barbs of the gale
as though it didn't know yet
it was dead, then it did,
and slipped slowly sideways
onto its own debris in the gutter.

4.

When Ivan Karamazov
is reciting his wracking disquisition
about the evils perpetrated
on children, opining whether
human salvation would be worth
a single child's suffering,
you know he's close to breaking
down, sobbing in shame
and remorse, and I wonder
if he'd imagined our whole planet,
the children with it,
wagered in a mad gamble
of world against wealth,
what would he have done?

5.

What do I do? Fret
mostly, and brood, and lie
awake. Not to sleep
wasn't always so punishing.
Once, in a train, stalled
in mountains, in snow,
I was wakened by the clank
of a trainman's crowbar
on the undercarriage of my car.
I lifted the leathery shade
and across a moon-dazzled
pine-fringed slope a fox
cut an arc; everything
else was pure light.

6.

I wanted it to last forever,
but I was twenty, and before
I knew it was back sleeping.
Do I ever sleep that way
now, innocent of everything
beyond my ken? No,
others are always with me,
others I love with my life,
yet I'll leave them scant
evidence of my care, and little
trace of my good intentions,
as little as the solacing shush
of the phantom limbs of our slain
tree will leave on the night.

GRACE CAVALIERI

(b. 1937)

∽

*Author of eleven books of poetry and twenty produced works for stage,
opera and film. She is the producer/host for public radio's "The Poet and
the Poem," on-air for twenty-five years and now broadcast from the Library
of Congress via NPR satellite. Born in New Jersey, she lives in Maryland.*

The Perfect Day

There was one moment when
the house floated among the trees
of Summer, maybe three o'clock,
when everything was warm
and smelled of powder, when
our mothers were in the kitchen
and it was perfectly still.
The sun in the afternoon
was lace on the street as
I stood clean and warm in a
white starched sundress. I did
not know what to call that feeling
. . . one moment of balance . . .
when the air was the same exact
temperature as my blood, smooth
inside and out. This was before
dinner time where there would
be iced tea and sliced cold
tomatoes, and the sound of a spoon
against the quiet table.

I think of that now as you lie
beside me asleep, wrapped in
a comforter of red and white,
as I watch the white snow
from the window rising to its trees
to hide a woodpecker, red
and white and black.
I think how one moment cannot be
another, how the perfect day
is gone from us with its sweet
second of comfort and how this, too,
is almost gone, how soon I will
lie in another perfect moment and
remember your breathing in the silence
today as I watched the birds eating
the suet from the kindness of that
feeding. And, years later, again,
how I will wish for another moment,
wishing back to this moment, reaching
further to the perfect moment when
I stood alone by the street.

Blue-Green Spirit

Oh Dream Wanderer
with your message stick
with your rooster crowing,

Where is the voice I spoke
after I was dead
before I was born?

How much has been left by the wayside?

If every dream were a tattoo
how would I look?

Would I start loving my skin
turning in the light
holding up my arm to understand
what each flower means?

They say because the female bird
can't sing
she flies only during Summer in Sweden,

Oh no, listen,
she is connected to the divine and
sings of her taste for life and death,

She sings until heard,
it is the voice we share where
nothing is lost.

A Classic Epic Begins

Swimming was for the long term
on the top edge of water.
What was underneath?

Happiness is a state of mind,
they told me, patting my bony
unformed hand, a fiction of caring—

A life of eggs extraordinaire;
here's the perfect diet, they said.

Whether there were plans for me
I did not know, and like most ignorant people
prided myself on my wisdom.

The first time I learned of fame
was when our aunt with
the spectacular breasts wrote
a death note, asking if at her
viewing they'd leave the
top of her dress unbuttoned.

To their meager credit, they did
and I am warmed by this,
the manufacture of charm.

ALICIA OSTRIKER

(b. 1937)

∞

She is the author of nine volumes of poetry, most recently The Little Space:
Poems Selected and New, 1968–1998. *She is also the author of two volumes
on women's poetry,* Writing Like a Woman *and* Stealing the Language: The
Emergence of Women's Poetry in America.

The Nature of Beauty

I can only say, there we have been; but I cannot say where.
— *T. S. Eliot*

As sometimes whiteness forms in a clear sky
To represent the breezy, temporary
Nature of beauty,
Early in semester they started it.
Lisa read in her rich New Jersey accent,
Which mixes turnpike asphalt with fast food,
A sexy poem that mentioned "the place
Where lovers go to when their eyes are closed
And their lips smiling." Other students grinned,
Thinking perhaps of the backseats of Hondas.
Instead of explaining "place" as a figure of speech,
The teacher wanted them to crystallize
Around it as around the seed of a cloud.
You all understand that? You understand?
The place we go to? Where we've been? They got it.

All semester they brought it back
A piece at a time, like the limbs of Osiris.
Mostly from sex, for they were all American
Nineteen to twenty-one year olds
Without a lot of complicated notions.
But Doug got it from the Jersey Shore,
Foam stroking his shins, his need
Leaping in fish form. Robin
One time from dancing
With a woman she didn't
Have sex with, once from her grandmother
Doing the crossword puzzle in pen.
Kindly David from a monstrous orange bus
Whose driver amazed him by kindliness
To passengers who were poor and demented.
Dylan from a Baptist church when song
Blent him into its congregation, sucked him
Into God, for a sanctified quarter hour,
"There's no separation at that height,"
Before it dropped him like Leda back to earth
And the perplexity of being white.

The vapor of the word collects,
Becomes cloud, pours itself out,
Almost before you think: the small
Rain down can rain.
A brief raid on the inarticulate
Is what we get, and in retreat we cannot
Tell where we've really been, much less remain.

Middle-Aged Woman at a Pond

The first of June, grasses already tall
In which I lie with a book. All afternoon a cardinal
Has thrown the darts of his song.

One lozenge of sun remains on the pond,
The high crowns of the beeches have been transformed
By a stinging honey. *Tell me,* I think.

Frogspawn floats in its translucent sacs.
Tadpoles rehearse their crawls.
Here come the blackflies now,

And now the peepers. This is the nectar
In the bottom of the cup,
This blissfulness in which I strip and dive.

Let my questions stand unsolved
Like trees around a pond. Water's cold lick
Is a response. I swim across the ring of it.

LAURA BOSS

(b. 1938)

∞

The founding editor of Lips, *author of four books of poetry, and winner of three poetry fellowships from the NJ State Council on the Arts, she represented the USA at the XXVI International Struga Poetry Readings in Yugoslavia in 1987.*

Airborne: Listening to the Reports of JFK Jr.'s Plane Missing After Leaving Caldwell Airport

Years ago, at Caldwell Airport,
    I left in a tiny plane
    my sixteen-year-old was piloting

The two of us in this one-engine seemingly
    "paper" plane he had pushed back with
    one hand while checking it before we left

I did not want to be in this plane,
    but it was just after I had separated
    from his father, and my guilt was
    making me try to please this son,
    I had so displeased by leaving his father

The guy I was going with at the time
    had put his gold cross around my neck
    and was crying as we left—though
    his fear would not let him come up with us

My son said I was brave—
    All his friends who had come up with him
    were either screaming or throwing up at this
    point in the trip

We circled over New York City
    We headed up to Maine where
    my older son was going to school—

There was no control tower person, but
    my son landed after a few more circles

Coming back from Maine that night
    my son told me to scan the horizon for planes
    too near to us

He told me I was right—
    He shouldn't be flying at night—that
    everything looked the same at night

He had me hold the map which he circled
    with his flashlight—trying to find out
    exactly where we were

I asked him if he had another battery for his
    flashlight—or, even another flashlight—
    He said, "No"

I told him, I'd buy him another flashlight when we
    got back

He told me if for any reason, he passes out
    or hits his head, I should click on a center
    radio station and they'd tell me how
    to fly the plane in

When we finally land, I ask him if his father has
    ever gone up with him
    "No," he replies, "He says he's not ready"
    (I'm not ready either I tell myself)
    and I think that my former husband
    is smarter than I thought he was

But I also think how women try to please males—
    to so often do things they don't want to do
    just to please a man—whether it be family or lover—

And, I think how Carolyn Bessette
    who according to the news and family reports
    did not want JFK Jr. to fly his own plane
    and how she and even her older sister tried to please him
    to show him that they did believe in him
    by climbing into that private plane

And I know how lucky I was when I got off that small
    one-engine plane at Caldwell Airport, so many years ago

And I think how unlucky those women were when
    leaving Caldwell Airport Friday night—
    that good intentions, guilt, and, yes, even love
    cannot always keep one airborne

JOYCE CAROL OATES

(b. 1938)

∞

Prolific poet, award-winning novelist and short-story writer, playwright,
critic, and editor. Born in upstate New York, she is Professor of English and
writing at Princeton University.

Sparrow Hawk above a New Jersey Cornfield

This hawk in silhouette
    a razor's edge
        weightless
            sheerly black
                innocent as a scrap of paper,
                    forked to sail—
                        the black-feathered muscles
                              scarcely moving,
                                  the eye
                                      unerring—
                          January winds
                      like waves washing
                  through the tallest trees—

                  We are crossing the snow-stubbled
                                  field
            in awe of
            that singular motion,
        flawless, seemingly
    idle—
Life hunting life—

And the Sunday sky a hard ceramic blue:
Splendid bird!—
all theology reduced
to a beaked silhouette
gliding, idly
turning
weightless
as an eye's casual mote—
But how splendid a bird!—
the eye
unerring—
now rising,
slowly banking,
circling,
and again soaring
as if it were a benediction of the air
and not life hunting life—

So the shadow of Death skims
lightly
the snow at our feet,
the beak hidden,
the silhouette taut
with grace,
innocence—
Splendid bird whose blood isn't pricked
by the sweet scent of ours—

Night Driving

South into Jersey on I-95, rain and
windshield wipers and someone you love asleep
in the seat beside you, light on all sides
like teeth winking and that smell like baking
bread gone wrong, and you want
to die it's so beautiful—
you love the enormous trucks floating in spray
and the tall smokestacks rimmed with flame
and this hammering in your head,
this magnet drawing what's deepest
in you you can't name
except to know it's there.

WILLIAM J. HIGGINSON
(b. 1938)

∞

*Returned to New Jersey in 2002 after eleven years in Santa Fe, New Mexico.
He is known worldwide mainly for his translations of and writings on
Japanese and international haiku, particularly* The Haiku Handbook *(1985)
and* Haiku World *(1996).*

one maple leaf
end over end on the sand
without a trace

crescent moon
would I look at the clouds
without it?

for Sachiyo Itô

moonlight glitters—
　　　the edge of a spread fan
　　　　　slices smoke

father dead
fifty years . . . I stare
into rank leaves

STEPHEN DUNN

(b. 1939)

∞

Author of thirteen books of poetry, including Different Hours *(winner of the 2001 Pulitzer Prize), Dunn taught at Richard Stockton College of New Jersey for thirty years, and now lives in Maryland.*

Achilles in Love

There was no getting to his weakness.
In public, even in summer, he wore
big boots, specially made for him,
a band of steel reinforcing each heel.
At home, when he bathed or slept,
he kept a pistol within reach, loaded.
And because to be invulnerable
is to be alone, he was alone even when
he was with you. You could sense it
in the rigidity of his carriage, as if under
his fine-fitting suits were layers of armor.
Yet everyone loved to see him in action:
While his enemies were thinking of small
advantages, he only thought end game.

Then she came along, who seemed to be all
women fused into one, cheek bones and breasts
evidence that evolution doesn't care
about fairness, and a mind so good, well,
it was like his. You could see his body soften
and days later, when finally they were naked
she instinctively knew what to do—
as smart men do with a mastectomy's scar—
to kiss his heel before kissing
what he considered to be his power,
and with a tenderness that made him tremble.

And so Achilles began to live differently.
Both friends and enemies were astounded
by his willingness to listen, and hesitate
before responding. Even in victory he'd
walk away without angering a single god.
He wore sandals now because she liked him in sandals.
He never felt so exposed, or so open to the world.
You could see in his face something resembling terror,
but in fact it was love, for which he would die.

A Postmortem Guide

For my eulogist, in advance

Do not praise me for my exceptional serenity.
Can't you see I've turned away
from the large excitements,
and have accepted all the troubles?

Go down to the old cemetery; you'll see
there's nothing definitive to be said.
The dead once were all kinds—
boundary breakers and scalawags,
martyrs of the flesh, and so many
dumb bunnies of duty, unbearably nice.

I've been a little of each.

And, please, resist the temptation
of speaking about virtue.
The seldom-tempted are too fond
of that word, the small-
spirited, the unburdened.
Know that I've admired in others
only the fraught straining
to be good.

Adam's my man and Eve's not to blame.
He bit in; it made no sense to stop.

Still, for accuracy's sake you might say
I often stopped,
that I rarely went as far as I dreamed.

And since you know my hardships,
understand they're mere bump and setback
against history's horror.
Remind those seated, perhaps weeping,
how obscene it is
for some of us to complain.

Tell them I had second chances.
I knew joy.
I was burned by books early
and kept sidling up to the flame.

Tell them that at the end I had no need
for God, who'd become just a story
I once loved, one of many
with concealments and late-night rescues,
high sentence and pomp. The truth is
I learned to live without hope
as well as I could, almost happily,
in the despoiled and radiant now.

You who are one of them, say that I loved
my companions most of all.
In all sincerity, say that they provided
a better way to be alone.

The Metaphysicians of South Jersey

Because in large cities the famous truths
already had been plumbed and debated,
the metaphysicians of South Jersey lowered
their gaze, just tried to be themselves.
They'd gather at coffee shops in Vineland
and deserted shacks deep in the Pine Barrens.
Nothing they came up with mattered
so they were free to be eclectic, and as odd
as getting to the heart of things demanded.
They walked undisguised on the boardwalk.
At the Hamilton Mall they blended
with the bargain-hunters and the feckless.
Almost everything amazed them,
the last hour of a county fair,
blueberry fields covered with mist.
They sought the approximate weight of sadness,
its measure and coloration. But they liked
a good ball game too, well pitched, lots of zeroes
on the scoreboard. At night when they lay down,
exhausted and enthralled, their spouses knew
it was too soon to ask any hard questions.
Come breakfast, as always, the metaphysicians
would begin to list the many small things
they'd observed and thought, unable to stop talking
about this place and what a world it was.

ROBERT PINSKY

(b. 1940)

∞

Prize winning translator of Dante's Inferno *and one of America's former Poets Laureate, frequently a guest poet on PBS, he was born in Long Branch and now teaches in Boston.*

The Figured Wheel

The figured wheel rolls through shopping malls and prisons,
Over farms, small and immense, and the rotten little downtowns.
Covered with symbols, it mills everything alive and grinds
The remains of the dead in the cemeteries, in unmarked graves and
    oceans.

Sluiced by salt water and fresh, by pure and contaminated rivers,
By snow and sand, it separates and recombines all droplets and
    grains,
Even the infinite sub-atomic particles crushed under the illustrated,
Varying treads of its wide circumferential track.

Spraying flecks of tar and molten rock it rumbles
Through the Antarctic station of American sailors and technicians,
And shakes the floors and windows of whorehouses for diggers and
    smelters
From Bethany, Pennsylvania to a practically nameless, semi-penal
    New Town

In the mineral-rich tundra of the Soviet northernmost settlements.
Artists illuminate it with pictures and incised mottoes

Taken from the Ten Thousand Stories and the Register of True
    Dramas.
They hang it with colored ribbons and with bells of many pitches.

With paints and chisels and moving lights they record
On its rotating surface the elegant and terrifying doings
Of the inhabitants of the Hundred Pantheons of major Gods
Disposed in iconographic stations at hub, spoke and
    concentric bands,

And also the grotesque demi-Gods, Hopi gargoyles and Ibo dryads.
They cover it with wind-chimes and electronic instruments
That vibrate as it rolls to make an all-but-unthinkable music,
So that the wheel hums and rings as it turns through the births of
    stars

And through the dead-world of bomb, fireblast and fallout
Where only a few doomed races of insects fumble in the smoking
    grasses.
It is Jesus oblivious to hurt turning to give words to the unrighteous,
And is also Gogol's feeding pig that without knowing it eats a baby
    chick

And goes on feeding. It is the empty armor of My Cid, clattering
Into the arrows of the credulous unbelievers, a metal suit
Like the lost astronaut revolving with his useless umbilicus
Through the cold streams, neither energy nor matter, that agitate

The cold, cyclical dark, turning and returning.
Even in the scorched and frozen world of the dead after the holocaust
The wheel as it turns goes on accreting ornaments.
Scientists and artists festoon it from the grave with brilliant

Toys and messages, jokes and zodiacs, tragedies conceived
From among the dreams of the unemployed and the pampered,
The listless and the tortured. It is hung with devices
By dead masters who have survived by reducing themselves
    magically

To tiny organisms, to wisps of matter, crumbs of soil,
Bits of dry skin, microscopic flakes, which is why they are called
    "great,"
In their humility that goes on celebrating the turning
Of the wheel as it rolls unrelentingly over

A cow plodding through car-traffic on a street in Iasi,
And over the haunts of Robert Pinsky's mother and father
And wife and children and his sweet self
Which he hereby unwillingly and inexpertly gives up, because it is

There, figured and pre-figured in the nothing-transfiguring wheel.

Jersey Rain

Now near the end of the middle stretch of road
What have I learned? Some earthly wiles. An art.
That often I cannot tell good fortune from bad,
That once had seemed so easy to tell apart.

The source of art and woe aslant in wind
Dissolves or nourishes everything it touches.
What roadbank gullies and ruts it doesn't mend
It carves the deeper, boiling tawny in ditches.

It spends itself regardless into the ocean.
It stains and scours and makes things dark or bright:
Sweat of the moon, a shroud of benediction,
The chilly liquefaction of day to night,

The Jersey rain, my rain, soaks all as one:
It smites Metuchen, Rahway, Saddle River,
Fair Haven, Newark, Little Silver, Bayonne.
I feel it churning even in fair weather

To craze distinction, dry the same as wet.
In ripples of heat the August drought still feeds
Vapors in the sky that swell to drench my state—
The Jersey rain, my rain, in streams and beads

Of indissoluble grudge and aspiration:
Original milk, replenisher of grief,
Descending destroyer, arrowed source of passion,
Silver and black, executioner, source of life.

MARIA MAZZIOTTI GILLAN

(b. 1940)

∞

*Founder and Director of the Poetry Center at Passaic County Community
College. Director of the Creative Writing Program at Binghamton
University-SUNY, she lives and teaches in New Jersey and is the author of
eight books of poetry.*

Mrs. Sinnegan's Dogwood

I

On this morning in May,
Mrs. Sinnegan's dogwood
suddenly blossoms all white lace,
a delicate tracery
that filters light.

Each spring, I watch this tree
for the moment of silver light
when the long sleep ends and the words
that have lain dormant in darkness
rise from ashes.

II

I remember the Japanese cherry tree that bowed
just outside my window; for years
the scent of blossoms perfumed my dreams.
I see the trees, the one inextricably woven
into the years of my growing; the other
tied to middle age, a double image,
iridescent and floating.

Mrs. Sinnegan drags her chair down her back steps,
one trembling hand on her walker,
the other pulling a metal lawn chair.
She positions her chair
so she can see the tree.
At eighty her bright eyes fade to pale blue,
and her words crawl.
Yet her heart
leaps through meadows
of clover and Queen Anne's lace.

III

This year, the dogwood blooms for weeks
like a special gift.
The leaves make patterns
on the roof. The birds gather
at the feeder and then perch on the edge
of my window, singing.
One day, Mrs. Sinnegan says the tree
looks like a girl in a communion veil;
another, like a bride pulling her satin train.
Today I imagine the tree is a matron
in a flowered hat.

THOMAS REITER

(b. 1940)

∞

Powers and Boundaries: Poems, his fourth book of poetry, was published by Louisiana State University Press in 2004. A native of Dubuque, Iowa, he is Wayne D. McMurray Professor of Humanities at Monmouth University in West Long Branch.

Rainbarrel

(To my grandmother)

Today I closed up your house,
having stayed with you that last night
when you called me by your mother's name
and the name of the son you lost
in childbirth. It took a long time
before I could touch those few flat curls
chemotherapy left. You awoke then
and you asked me to come with you
to the rainbarrel—only those few words,
but they made a place for me
in the madness of your dying, a small boy
balancing a pail on the barrel's rim
to draw for the first time what had fallen
as he slept, the sweet water you loved

for washing your long, unbraided hair.
But he cried out and jumped back:
in the eaves reflected there
he had seen a wasp crawling over its nest
beside his head. You laughed and taught him
how those blue-black daubers build,
you had him listen to the humming as
she troweled pellets of mud, a kind of singing
with nothing to fear in it,
vibrations to keep the earth
soft for molding. Sitting up with you
that last night I dreamt that cell by cell
a nest came building back to us,
but when I jostled and dissolved it
to draw out water, the blue-black song
came with me into the house
and you ladled it over my bowed head.

Going into the Barrens

These patches of lichen are,
like joy, the foliage
of stones, their roots in
tea-colored bogs and ponds

where the trail plays out
among cedar and pepperbush,
minutes from cardboard sopping
in dumpsters behind the mall.

A pool turns up with a view
of pods and scraps of chrysalis
only water on its way
back out of sight could hold.

Let the Barrens take your measure.
Today song is carrying
the forest's understory,
and you have grounds for listening:

spring chorus frogs, their call
like carpenters pounding nails
and building, over and over,
this place you can come back to.

Dragonfly

It was nose into a juniper
along the creek, and anyone
could look right through:
head, thorax, abdomen
hollow but whole,
wings open and untorn.
I carried that weightlessness
home to a bookshelf and
forgot it there.

Today, coming back with fall
grasses for the hand lens,
I found it again. The field guide
tells how the meat-eater of the stream bed
climbs a cattail in May,
how plated skin splits like a pod;
and how, still pale and damp,
a dragonfly waits astride itself
to mate in flight and die.

Old Mosquito Hawk,
you are worthy of time in the air.
Wings veined with mica, klieg eyes—
what blue forays they promise,
your eggs long broadcast on the water.

PENNY HARTER

(b. 1940)

∞

Returned to New Jersey in 2002 after eleven years in Santa Fe; she is the author of many volumes of poetry, including Lizard Light: Poems from the Earth *(1991) and* Buried in the Sky *(2001).*

Lizard Light

The lizard on our sidewalk
has no tail again; by tomorrow
a new tail will be budding
from the blunt stump, while
in the yard's tall grasses
ants will share the piece
our cat abandoned.

Each month the moon is a lizard,
angles of sunlight biting it down
and giving it back until someday
the sun goes dark.

If my limbs were stars
they would burn across light years,
their fire still living
no matter when they sputtered down
to bone and ash;

but now I guard this lizard
who plays dead between my feet,
the light already shining
from its wound.

JIM HABA

(b. 1940)

∽

Director of the Poetry Program at the Geraldine R. Dodge Foundation, he
organizes Dodge Poets in the Schools and designs and produces the biennial
Geraldine R. Dodge Poetry Festival.

Yes

Yes, the news is bad and getting worse.

Yes, we sometimes dream that even the angels feel
uncertain, isolated, peripheral, impotent.

Still, what we come to know
almost always proves different from
and so much more than
what we thought we knew.

Will we see them if we awaken?
Will we know them if we ascend?

DANIELA GIOSEFFI
(b. 1941)

∞

*Founder of Skylands Writers and Artists Association, Inc., National Book Award-winning author and editor, critic, novelist and poet (*Eggs in the Lake, *Boa Editions), she was born and raised in New Jersey and now lives in Brooklyn.*

Beyond the East Gate

I listen to the voice of the cricket,
loud in the quiet night,
warning me
not to mistake a hill for a mountain.
I need to be alone,
in a private house with doors that open only outward,
safe from strangers who smell of death,
where I can draft a universe under my eyelids
and let nothing invade it.

I want to sing a fugue
sounding like the genius of flowers
talking to leaves on their stems,
to have more concrete meaning
than even the dance of a child in my uterus.
I'm a lost and primitive priestess
wandering in a walled city of the wrong century.
I need to spend thirty years in the desert
before I will understand the sun,
thirty years at sea
to gather the blessing of salt and water.

In the back room of my skull
a secret dice game determines
the rites of my hands
before they touch flesh again.
I want to reach a peace I've never known,
to be an old woman who is very young,
a child who is a sage
come down from the mountain.

TOI DERRICOTTE

(b. 1941)

∽

A former resident of Montclair now teaching poetry at the University of Pittsburgh, she is author of Natural Birth *(Firebrand, 2000),* Tender *(1997) and* Captivity *(1995, University of Pittsburgh Press). She is co-founder of Cave Canem, the workshop/retreat for African-American poets.*

In Knowledge of Young Boys

i knew you before you had a mother,
when you were newtlike, swimming,
a horrible brain in water.
i knew you when your connections
belonged only to yourself,
when you had no history
to hook on to,
barnacle,
when you had no sustenance of metal
when you had no boat to travel
when you stayed in the same
place, treading the question;
i knew you when you were all
eyes and a cocktail,
blank as the sky of a mind,
a root, neither ground nor placental;
not yet
red with the cut nor astonished
by pain, one terrible eye
open in the center of your head
to night, turning, and the stars

blinked like a cat. we swam
in the last trickle of champagne
before we knew breastmilk—we
shared the night of the closet,
the parasitic
closing on our thumbprint,
we were smudged in a yellow book.

son, we were oak without
mouth, uncut, we were
brave before memory.

STEPHEN DOBYNS

(b. 1941)

∞

Born in Orange, he has taught writing at many universities and is now on
the faculty of the Sarah Lawrence MFA program. Author of twelve volumes
of poetry, a collection of essays on writing, and nearly two dozen novels and
short story collections, his latest book of poems is Mystery, So Long
(Penguin, 2005). He lives in Rhode Island where he writes a column for The
Westerly Times.

The Gardener

After the first astronauts reached heaven
the only god discovered in residence
retired to a little brick cottage
in the vicinity of Venus. He was not
unduly surprised. He had seen it coming
since Luther. Besides, what with the imminence
of nuclear war, his job was nearly over.
As soon as the fantastic had become
a commonplace, bus tours were organized,
and once or twice a day the old fellow
would be trotted out from his reading of Dante
and asked to do a few tricks—lightning bolts,
water sprouting from a rock, blood from a turnip.
A few of the remaining cherubim
would fly in figure eights and afterward
sell apples from the famous orchard.
In the evening, the retired god would sometimes
receive a visit from his old friend the Devil.
They would smoke their pipes before the fire.

The Devil would stroke his whiskers and cover
his paws with his long furry tail. The mistake,
he was fond of saying, was to make them in
your image instead of mine. Possibly, said
the ex-deity. He hated arguing. The mistake,
he had often thought, was to experiment
with animal life in the first place when
his particular talent was as a gardener.
How pleasant Eden had been in those early days
with its neat rows of cabbages and beets,
flowering quince, a hundred varieties of rose.
But of course he had needed insects, and then
he made the birds, the red ones which he loved;
later came his experiments with smaller mammals—
squirrels and moles, a rabbit or two. When
the temptation had struck him to make something
really big, he had first conceived of it
as a kind of scarecrow to stand in the middle
of the garden and frighten off predators. What
voice had he listened to that convinced him
to give the creature his own face? No voice
but his own. It had amused him to make
a kind of living mirror, a little homunculus
that could learn a few of his lesser tricks.
And he had imagined sitting in the evening
with his friend the Devil watching the small
human creatures frolic in the grass. They would
be like children, good-natured and always singing.
When had he realized his mistake? Perhaps
when he smiled down at the first and it
didn't smile back; when he reached down to help
it to its feet and it shrugged his hand aside.
Standing up, it hadn't walked on the paths marked
with white stones but on the flowers themselves.

It's lonely, God had said. So he made it a mate,
then watched them feed on each other's bodies,
bicker and fight and trample through his garden,
dissatisfied with everything and wanting to escape.
Naturally, he hadn't objected. Kicked out,
kicked out, who had spread such lies? Shaking
and banging the bars of the great gate, they had
begged him for the chance to make it on their own.

LOIS MARIE HARROD

(b. 1942)

∞

Her six books of poetry include Spelling the *World* Backwards *(Palanquin Press, 2000), and* Part of the Deeper Sea *(1997). A former Supervisor of Creative Writing at the New Jersey Governor's School of the Arts, she teaches English.*

Horseshoe Crabs

Brigantine Wildlife Refuge, 1992

It was not my day for love or death,
    and so I felt aloof, distant,
watching the horseshoe crabs

churn the bottom of their sandy basin
    as if the shore were a halfway house
and not part of the deeper sea.

The gulls too were there, black-headed
    and cackling, but they moved away,
scared from their own observations

when we stopped, you and I, to watch.
    Are they mating, you asked,
tens and twelves of crumpled shells

grinding over each other as if
    they were World War I helmets
deprived of bodies and so

in some platonic fashion were seeking one other
　　as cerebral as themselves.
Then we noticed their widely spaced eyes

riding their carapaces like small glass beads
　　seeming to see what they were banging
from any angle, and their spikes rising

at the base of their cephalothorax like toy cannons.
　　They did not seem to be hurting themselves,
though as I watched them, bouncing off each other

like bumper cars at a carnival,
　　making curious glubbing sounds
as if the brain's glue were dolloping out of a cranial case,

I thought of the way my cerebrum seems to sound,
　　separated from my body and living on its own,
as it does after we have been making love or fighting

and all my affection crawls off to a dented pot
　　in the kitchen drawer.
I remembered then that they are arthropods

twisted out of the same armor that we were twisted once
　　and I remember that afternoon and that night
our son, and then our daughter, were conceived,

how even as my own small body made
　　its smaller, unpredictable shudder,
that this time, death had some purpose

and perhaps the steel tanks shearing across the sand
    had some purpose too, though nothing
I could claim, so we walked on, the gulls descending

to tear at the crabs that had bellied-up on the shore,
    the ones that could not return to the water
except as some sporadic heckling.

The Mist

If metaphor
were sufficient,
I would think of mist today
as a silent woman
wrapping her body
around the noise of trees.

But I want to know
how she mutes
everything,
makes the world
subservient
to self,
that sweet
almost translucent
fog of being.

I want to know
how she lays herself
on thorns and thistles
muck and morass,
that place where
the deer breathed
and breathed no more,
how she pulls down
the firmament
and leaves it
hanging in the air
without a voice.

FRANK FINALE

(b. 1942)

∽

Essayist and anthologist, he is currently the Poetry Editor of the new renais-
sance. *Author of* To The Shore Once More, Volumes I and II *(Jersey Shore
Publications, 1999–2002).*

City Girls at Seaside Heights

They come again this summer, bare-legged
girls with boys under their asses,
to try and grab a piece
of the sun. The rum in their tropical
drinks blossoms their cheeks, their dreams
grow verdant in August; they move
their tans over the dark cracks
of the boardwalk, to the rhythm of steel
vibrations on dance floors or behind
the shine of dark glasses and ice-white
smiles. Like salmon running upstream
to spawn, they flash their tails,
till all their bubble and boil expends
itself leaving plastic bottles and reeds
of straws—the bones of their dollars
and time dissolving on the sand.

The Pond

Before we came, she told us how they dug
a bowl of earth about fifteen meters
in diameter, lined it with heavy plastic
and put in a channel eight meters deep.
Those years, she would seek out swamps, inlets,
other waters for life she needed:
arrow arrum, water lilies, blue flag.
She stocked it with goldfish and tadpoles.
In summer, huge-eyed darning needles would stitch
patterns above the reeds. Water striders,
quick as the spots before your eyes, skated
its filmy surface. Once her husband built
a bridge, curved, with closely spaced slats—
an Oriental eyelid. Spiders would weave
their webs between lid and lashes of reeds.
At night, the eye of the pond would reflect moon
and trees. Through July and August, frogs quonking
in the barrel of night would wake her.

The first winter we lived there,
after the divorce, the river hardened,
cars went tobogganing, Florida
had snow in its palms. The goldfish
froze. A white iron set the contours
of the garden brittling leaves and limbs.
She remarried, sent her daughter to college.

Less wide-eyed with water, its reflection
broken by too many weeds, the eye could barely
see lilies wilting, turtles giving way
to toads. It sprang a leak the summer
water was precious. Hidden by reeds
in the garden's corner, it waited. She called
telling how hard it was to find a job.
She would go back to work in another field.

Five summers passed before we freed the pond,
pulling weeds, filling it with water, restocking:
arrow arrum, water lilies, blue flag.
In another field, she found love and work.
We repaired the bridge. Standing, one night,
we caught our reflection with moon and stars.

Late July. A leopard lily purring
orange-red, all its spots showing, sprang up.
The frogs quonked deep into the night.

Ruffed Grouse

Drummer, I hear you each spring
courting the Connecticut hens to come
to the hemlock groves and alder runs
where you turn your feathered motor up
looking for some familiar tail.

EMANUEL DI PASQUALE

(b. 1943)

⚭

Living in New Jersey since 1968, he teaches at Middlesex County College. His books of poems include Genesis *(BOA Editions Limited, 1989) and* The Silver Lake Love Poems *(Bordighera, 2000). Awarded The Bordighera Poetry Prize (1998), The Academy of American Poets' Raiziss/de Palchi Fellowship (2000), and the Chelsea Award for Poetry (2002).*

Extended Memory (Sicily)

I

When it was time to ride the horse, I said to my friend,
George, "I'm afraid. You ride it. I'll ride the donkey."
And as the horse took George quickly through the mossy valley,
I followed on the donkey.

At the farm, the women were hurling wheat up the sky.
The wind made clouds of chaff. Wheat fell like rain.
George had picked peaches and prunes and gave me a handful.

Strawberry scents filling a small roadway—
figs, pomegranates, mulberries.

II

My grandfather talked in his sleep—a mason's jargon.
He'd huff and puff and swing his pick in his sleep.
Oh, my grandmother's fears!

III

After my father died, my mother insisted we had ghosts
in the house. She saw a dove flutter and vanish
into the ceiling. For her, candles lowered or shot out
their flames. She heard door knocks no one else heard.
And my father stayed dead.

Always Finish with a Poem

Always finish with a poem
in praise of children;
mention their eyes,
open and giving; the sun
and moon and beetle stare,
the hungry wolf,
and ocean with currents without end—
the sure look that,
fully realizing objects
one by one,
doesn't rush or blur.
Mention their limbs
that easily somersault.
Praise their dreams
of birds' songs
in restless dawns
and rain slipping
down tree trunks
in those twilights cradled
in a father's gathering arms
or the warm nest of a mother.
Praise the children
for their ready tears.
And praise the children
for their belly laughs,
their unstopped throats.

Turkey Duck

I look for you as I circle the lake,
red-faced, grotesque, old turkey duck,
Canadian geese stand like long-rooted trees
while you, lonely and lowly,
squat behind them
like a midget bush.

I remember a few days ago
the boy—curly haired, blonde
handsome youngster—cursing at you:
"Get away, you're ugly, ugly," he yelled,
and would not throw you bread.
And I recall how you stood back
and stared at the brown earth.

But to me, dear friend,
you're beautiful—
my children bring you bread.
I wonder where your friends are,
your family, bumpy-headed,
turkey-faced and handsome-red.
I sing you a prayer, shy grubber,
and make your loneliness mine.
We both breathe cool autumn winds
and share the full moon chill
and leftover bread.

DANIEL ZIMMERMAN

(b. 1945)

⚭

Teaches English at Middlesex County College in Edison, New Jersey. His dissertation (SUNY at Buffalo, 1984) explored the poetics of William Blake. A former editor of College English Notes *for the New Jersey College English Association, he has published several collections of poetry, most recently* Post-Avant *(Columbus, OH: Pavement Saw Press, 2001).*

Last Breath

if I could burst into flame, fire with fire,
if a tongue of flame would rise, eloquent,
over my head, to quench the smoldering,
underground black veins of anthropocide;

if I could flood a fuselage with words,
water to drown witches & float the rest
to Ararat, emblem of all ships since,
reverse the way witches always get tried;

if earth itself would gnaw & devour
the lines on maps & not plow lines on flesh,
if air could deny the airfoil lift
lifting a secret hell into the sky;

the heart would break still, but break to unite;
platitude turn proverb, hater relent.

SANDER ZULAUF

(b. 1946)

∽

His first collection of poems, Succasunna New Jersey, *was published in 1987 (Breaking Point). He is Professor of English at County College of Morris, Randolph, founding editor,* Index of American Periodical Verse *(1971–1982), and editor of the* Journal of New Jersey Poets *(1989–present). Named first Poet Laureate, Episcopal Diocese of Newark, 1999.*

Where Time Goes

Look, there's a picture of my little sister,
Age three, on her red tricycle, bright
Blonde hair, eyes squinting in the sunlight,
She's fifty now, and there's
One of my son, age one,
In the arms of my mom,
Both sharing
A genuine laugh together, she's fifty two
In the picture, and would live
Until he was six. He's nearing thirty now,
Look, there's a Christmas tree,
A summer vacation at the Lake,
Three of us before the 1964
World's Fair Globe and Shea,
Old Timer's Day at Yankee Stadium,
A wedding, a baptism,
An anniversary, Niagara Falls,
No new cars in this family,
A carved steaming turkey, one dog,
Most looking happy and healthy,

Some looking slightly angry, some afflicted,
Some looking disappointed,
A crowd gathered outside a church
Waiting for the groom, the bride,
These pictures have reached equilibrium
Where there is now one dead in them
For every one still living,
And soon, soon,
Even the immortal in these images
Will be very old, unable to recognize
Anyone, then gone, and these pictures
Will be thrown away and everything
Very priceless will be as unseen
As the earth miles beneath you, dark
As the fathomless space between
Three bright stars,
All the love shed,
The hearts silent.

Jersey Lightning

For days the electrician
Has been making mayhem
Replacing wiring in the basement,
Living room and bedrooms,
And has now, 350 lbs of him, squeezed
Like toothpaste up through the crawl space
Into the attic and round the bend
Working on the junction boxes.
And now the kids come downstairs
Into the kitchen telling me
They've heard someone yelling for help
And I immediately see him
Stuck forever in the attic. I climb
The stepladder, stick my head through,
Repeatedly yell his name.
No answer.
I begin to shake with visions
Of emergency crews, cherry pickers,
And a hole in the roof to raise him up.
I tell the kids to go downstairs and call for help.
Then, from far back in the cave,
He lumbers around the corner
Coated with flecks of cellulose
Insulation, holding a drop light,
Asking me to throw him a few
Wire nuts.

Elegy for Wally

Nastiest little love bird
That ever hatched
Bit me once a week
Hook-billed shriek
Drew blood from the hand
That fed her.
Got her from the Noah's Ark
Animal Shelter for free
Eight years ago, a he,
We thought, until she laid
An egg and broke it.
Tried to give her a wicker nest
She ripped apart,
So got her an old bean soup can
She'd pull over herself
For naps and sleep.
Let her out of her cage,
She'd tear up books and papers,
Shove the long strips in her butt,
Strut around the floor
Bite at anything in range
Cleaned her cage, new food,
Fresh water, fresh sprigs of millet,
Still got bit.
Aging she began to pull out
All her feathers, turning on herself
After we learned to keep our distance
Until that day I found her
On the cage floor breathing rapidly,
A sneeze, gave her some drops of water
On her beak, she began flapping
Her wings trying desperately

To out-fly death,
And the world in the cage
Came to a standstill.
I took the cage apart,
Wrapped her in towels,
Put her in her can
With a sprig of millet,
Her plastic bird pal Buddy
Whom she liked humping,
Sent her off to the afterlife
Like a royal Egyptian
Sailing toward Orion's Belt,
Wrapped her in her
Cage drying towel,
Buried her near
The bird bath outside
Down below the deck
She'd freely roam
Long lazy summer afternoons
Biting at our toes, our ankles,
Drawing blood on days nobody'd
Give a thought to death at all,
Only killing.

CHARLES H. JOHNSON

(b. 1947)

∞

*He is a 2004 Paterson Poetry Prize finalist for his new book of poems enti-
tled* Tunnel Vision. *A 1998 Allen Ginsberg Poetry Awards first-place winner,
he is a Geraldine R. Dodge Foundation poet and poetry editor for the online
literary magazine* Identity Theory.

A Tragedy

It feels good to put words on paper,
to tap out your life's SOS
through the only keys that can save you.

Someone will be listening for your rhythmic cry
echoing up through lines that gasp for air
just below the surface.

A poet must set his course
to overtake Odysseus and lead the warrior king
back home.

A journey not in years
but in lifetimes spent sailing to Penelope
before remembering his kingdom

is in the belly of a horse at Troy
and only Helen is worth living—
and even dying—for.

The Old West

A little brown boy sat on the top step
of the front stoop to his family's row house
in West Philadelphia and dreamed of a world
that wasn't passing him by. His very best
friend across the street sat on the top
step of the front stoop to his family's
row house and waited for the world
to catch up to him. When either boy got
permission to cross the street they played
all the parts they'd seen on television
that week. The best ones were all action
with only "Yup" or "Nope" or "Be seein'
ya, pardner" to fill in the gaps between
fights with imaginary bad guys or Indians.
When the little brown boy asked his dad
for a cap pistol he'd seen on TV that week
he was told to "forget all that nonsense
because everybody knows there weren't any
colored cowboys or soldiers in the Old West."
But since a boy's gotta do what a man's
gotta do, whenever a little brown boy could
cross the street another desperado would bite
the dust and the cavalry would ride to
the rescue for all the colored people to see
from the windows and porches and front stoops
of their row houses in West Philadelphia.

YUSEF KOMUNYAKAA

(b. 1947)

☙

*Yusef Komunyakaa wrote the most acclaimed book of American poetry about
the Vietnam War,* Dien Cai Dau *(1988). Like Wilfred Owen and other modern
war poets, Komunyakaa is attentive to inner experience and to shared politi-
cal history. "My belief is that you have to have both," he remarked in an
interview, "the odyssey outward as well as inward" (Callaloo, 1990).*

Venus's-flytraps

I am five,
    Wading out into deep
      Sunny grass.
Unmindful of snakes
    & yellowjackets, out
      To the yellow flowers
Quivering in sluggish heat.
    Don't mess with me
      'Cause I have my Lone Ranger
Six-shooter. I can hurt
    You with questions
      Like silver bullets.
The tall flowers in my dreams are
    Big as the First State Bank,
      & they eat all the people
Except the ones I love.
    They have women's names,
      With mouths like where
Babies come from. I am five.
    I'll dance for you

If you close your eyes. No
Peeping through your fingers.
I don't supposed to be
This close to the tracks.
One afternoon I saw
What a train did to a cow.
Sometimes I stand so close
I can see the eyes
Of men hiding in boxcars.
Sometimes they wave
& holler for me to get back. I laugh
When trains make the dogs
Howl. Their ears hurt.
I also know bees
Can't live without flowers.
I wonder why Daddy
Calls Mama honey.
All the bees in the world
Live in little white houses
Except the ones in these flowers.
All sticky & sweet inside.
I wonder what death tastes like.
Sometimes I toss the butterflies
Back into the air.
I wish I knew why
The music in my head
Makes me scared.
But I know things
I don't supposed to know.
I could start walking
& never stop.
These yellow flowers
Go on forever.
Almost to Detroit.

Almost to the sea.
    My mama says I'm a mistake.
        That I made her a bad girl.
My playhouse is underneath
    Our house, & I hear people
        Telling each other secrets.

Ambush

So quiet birds
start singing again.
Lizards bring a touch of light.
The squad leader counts bullets
a third time. Stars
glint off gunbarrels.
We can almost hear a leaf
falling. "For chrissake. Please."
Raw opium intoxicates
a blaze of insects.
Buddhist monks on a hill
burn twelve red lanterns.
"Put out your stupid cigarette,
PFC," the Recon corporal whispers.
The trees play games.
A tiger circles us, in his broken cage
between sky & what's human.
"We'll wait out the bastards.
They have to come this way,
& when they do, not
even God can help 'em."
Headless shadows skirt the hedgerow.
A crossroad for lost birds
calling to the dead,
& then a sound that makes you jump
in your sleep years later,
the cough of a mortar tube.

Facing It

My black face fades,
hiding inside the black granite.
I said I wouldn't,
dammit: No tears.
I'm stone. I'm flesh.
My clouded reflection eyes me
like a bird of prey, the profile of night
slanted against morning. I turn
this way—the stone lets me go.
I turn that way—I'm inside
the Vietnam Veterans Memorial
again, depending on the light
to make a difference.
I go down the 58,022 names,
half-expecting to find
my own in letters like smoke.
I touch the name Andrew Johnson;
I see the booby trap's white flash.
Names shimmer on a woman's blouse
but when she walks away
the names stay on the wall.
Brushstrokes flash, a red bird's
wings cutting across my stare.
The sky. A plane in the sky.
A white vet's image floats
closer to me, then his pale eyes
look through mine. I'm a window.
He's lost his right arm
inside the stone. In the black mirror
a woman's trying to erase names:
No, she's brushing a boy's hair.

JOE SALERNO

(1947 – 1995)

∽

*Won the Hopwood Award at the University of Michigan in the early 1970s.
He died at age 48. Posthumous publication of two books,* Dream Paintings
from the Heaven of Obscurity *and* Only Here, *was accomplished by a group
of the poet's friends.*

In The Dark

With his head
On my shoulder, my newborn son
Has fallen asleep. In the dark,
I hold him there, resting
My cheek on his forehead—a violinist
Who has put down his bow
And stands quietly overwhelmed
By his own music.

Moose Love

Almost shyly
the large male moves
slowly towards her,
his love
a patient bawling
of desire. He waits
with his big eyes open and calm,
days sometimes, for her
leisurely acquiescence
to his need.

He shakes from time to time
the two immense wings of his antlers,
rattling dry brush
and scraping the bark of trees;
a tense serenade, as she
walks on ahead,
her inviting rump flagrantly
casual of his arousal.

Only then, after such
meek pursuit and love-wandering,
finally, in the high weeds
of autumn, will she let him mount;
his great shaggy patience
brimming over into awkward passion,
as each long pulse of seed
fills her quietly
and she wears above her
the vast triumphal
wavering of his crown.

DAVID SHAPIRO

(b. 1947)

∞

Born in Newark, the author of nine books of poetry (including A Burning
Interior, *2002) and several critical studies, the recipient of many major
fellowships and the 1977 Morton Dauwen Zabel Poetry Award from the
American Academy of Arts and Letters, he now resides in New York. He once
defined poetry this way: "We're all crying 'Help!' in 47 languages."*

The Seasons

In Memory of John Cage

SUMMER

I saw the ruins of poetry,
Of a poetry
Of a parody and it was
Terraces and gardens
A mural bright as candy
With unconcealed light
The ceiling sprayed upon us
With a bit of the Atlantic
Fish leaping about a henotheism
That permits no friend
And leaves us happier
In the sand than in our room
You are not a little bird in the street
Protected by a stationary car
And protesting too little

Synthesize the aqueduct and
The tepidarium and the lion's pit
The sun stapled shut
The sun not a wandering error
Sunspots are hair
Sun from above or in the light's maw
The sun as a windshield and we drove to time's beach
The sun another snowman
A monkey for a child
Unkidnapped calm
Good day! good time! pulverized shore
At night, when everyone is writing
At night, when everyone is reading
Or learning to read in the dark
Time, with its patent pending
Half-eaten fruit of those
Who fear no lions
No weapons
No suspects, no motives
Walking down the beach on
Our heads: man and dog
Forced alike to swim in hurricanes
By the father, actually to dog paddle
Without a subject like a fireweed
Or a thistle
But the law we did not abide and carried by air
A single drop and I mean drop
Of a honeysuckle would satisfy me then
A cricket arises at the bottom of the lawn
Alone and vague it hesitates to mount the curb
A natural fire discovered in the grillework of these woods
The long column of summer days
Scornfully you lower all the eyelids
And we breathe together a long time

AUTUMN

A project and a lack of derealization
And a warehouse like a button
A façade in dark gray velvet
With strips of false marble lettering
Bending with the remover to remove
Absorbed into the sky like a gourd
My temporary window like a garden
And the stairwell split open
Into the interior view of a sieve
Of stairwells elaborate in cross section
And the axiometric of Charles Lindbergh
A mannikin feted in his aviator clothes
At the Salon of Autumn
With your hands full of women's
Accessories
And the President with his lips
In the frigidaires
And the tires rolling up at the annual
Automobile salon
Something enormous: the real estate
You did not buy
Sun spots bleeding beneath an oak
No floor
No young fate
The history of time-lapse photography
Is falling now
You cannot even take dictation like daughters
You have destroyed a little of everything
How dare you interrupt my house
Of empty pictures
Make music too loud to listen to
Want the bed too low

Don't want this to exist
Want me to become unconscious
Of too many colors

A house to sink
Violins without bridges
Pencils too heavy to be carried
Dictionaries stuck in the ground
And the violin lies on the long black piano and replies

WINTER

Hard winter
Unlivable house
Unlivable snow
It is true January
However
My son is smiling in his sleep
After death there are extremes
Of temperature
An automobile is attached to the planet
And it sails the ice like a caravel
It is a word without songs
And one stops on the highway
To observe the snow's perspective
As the executions are executed
With a technical precision
Like Ricci's spicatti
And the dead slide sidewise
While the moon moves outward
Failing to grip the roadway
Like a bed sliding under the frame
Of a cloudless sky

February has clumped and intimated
That I find you in these halls
Of powerlessness
The fields are messier each day
Freezing water throttles the sky
We are idle, like a pair
Of wild cars on the highway
O northern widowed word
Ice like a sidewalk on the river
A difficult year
And the head emits a hot kind of hope
The truth a novel highway going round
The suburbs and ultimately I
Become part of myself not you and a gulf and sea
Held at precise angles to forbid us
Crypto-opponents to join
In natural darkness
Whose tied feet the imaginary rat gnawed through
In comatose sleep I saw you last
No cemetery holds you nor a single
Fire that I could burn
I pretend to approach your metal mouth,
You put it close to me
Brush your lips with ice
In a key he rarely chose the F sharp minor
You used to say Oh you could say anything

SPRING

A boy who stayed awake
And what he saw
Very near as opposed to
To the west of everything

He kisses the bug
The charred blossoms of the dogwood
Family sculpture or
Family carving
My father would point to the
Anomalous forsythia
Because of this truthless
Encyclopedism
It is just as good to meet
A dog or a cat
What they left out: Anger
Sex and history
My grandfather died singing
Called the best death
As my father stayed at the music stand
Or the dancer wants to do
That new thing: dancing until the end
A construction site in sunlight
I had written: Superbia's loutish
Psychological best-of-horse show
Does your promise shine like a highway
Like an effaced green work on a wall
Singing and partly singing
I walked with my son a little way
I say good-bye but not enough
He whirls around I disappear
You need the shadow of a child
Like an avalanche
He was glad he had stayed awake
And he stayed awake to this day
You the chrysalis and I the traditional ancestor exploded
      like aluminum

DRAWING AFTER SUMMER

I saw the ruins of poetry, of a poetry
Of a parody and it was a late copy bright as candy.
I approach your metal mouth, you put it close to me.

By the long column of a summer's day
Like a pair of wild cars on the highway
I saw the ruins of poetry, of a poetry.

The doll within the doll might tell the story
Inside the store: the real estate you could not buy.
I approach your metal mouth, you put it close to me.

Violin lies on piano and makes reply.
Hunted words. Gathered sentences. Pencils too heavy to carry.
I saw the ruins of poetry, of a poetry.

The history of time-lapse photography
Is a student exercise. Throttle the sky.
I approach your metal mouth, you put it close to me.

The moon moves outward failing to grip the roadway.
I see you stuck in the ground like a dictionary.
I saw the ruins of poetry, of a poetry.
I approach your metal mouth, you put it close to me.

ROCHELLE RATNER

(b. 1948)

∞

She is the author of fourteen poetry collections and two novels and Executive Editor of American Book Review. *Her anthology,* Bearing Life: Women's Writings on Childlessness, *was published by The Feminist Press.*

Person With A Mask On

I.

I tell you I'm from Atlantic City.
Then I go on to explain
that I'm from Margate,
a suburb where most
of the richer people live.

Already I've given
more of myself
than you realize.

You should visit here—
you'll understand me,
you'll know why I'm shy at times
and bold
almost arrogant
at other times.

You'll find traces of me
in alleys behind buildings
or vacant lots
where buildings were torn down.
You'll find traces in the traffic lights
each corner.

Laughing,
I say again
this is where I came from.
Always past tense.
I speak as if this town and I
were separate.

II.

Look for what's missing.
You'll see the weeds
that I picked
as a child
and gave my mother

the weeds
that I kept for myself

the weeds I didn't pick
one year
because I found
a building had been built there—

the yellow brick school
we lived next door to.
It was a part of me also.

They promised my parents
when we bought
our house
they didn't have plans to build
for at least ten years.

This was four years later.
No more weeds left.

III.

Look at those waves
out there along the ocean.
Since you can't take one
and hold it in your hand
you say it's not real.

We speak of the ocean
as calm today.
I speak of myself
with a headache or an earache.
Like the wave
it won't be real without me.

You see a pigeon
rushing toward the food
I offer up.
But what if I didn't throw it,
just made motions,
my arm
reaching toward my pocket
emerging fist closed
gesturing to air?

He would still dart against me.
And the other birds
would think I'd fed him.

Everyone complains
about those pigeons.
Nests on buildings.
Crap around you
everywhere you look.

IV.

I speak of myself as a bird.
But you understand what I'm saying.

Bird, city, me.
The old lighthouse
now painted red
where it used to be blue

my grandfather's house
so large I can't remember
all the rooms,
with a third floor
that I've never even seen
(he lives alone there now
ever since his wife died)

my father's office
which he keeps expanding

the boat ride we took
around the island
and the men who begged for coins
along the boardwalk.

I show you my grandfather's house,
my father's office.
Nothing more.
I give you my hand,
bent at the wrist.

I brought you here
to show you parts of things.
Like a jigsaw puzzle.
Only this time
nothing fits together.

The city stays the same.
It's we who change it.
We tear down an old hotel
to build a new one;
we call an old place
by a modern name.

We never think about landmarks.
Or if we do
we want them to be
the way that waves are.
Distorting shape and form.
Always of interest.

The First Day on Feverfew

Today my skull was cleansed,
lifted gently out
of the body,
held in the mountain stream
letting still-wintry waters
wash over it.
I opened it, rinsed inside,
used a small gold brush
to get at all the crevices.
If only I could articulate
how different it feels now,
but you, you see skulls
as trophies
hanging on the wall
of some hunting lodge.
I can't begin to show you pain
or explain its absence
even to myself.
Settle for this skull, then,
newly discovered on some
forest path, not killed,
just found there,
free of dirt and blood now,
pure white and resting gently
on these shoulders you like
to drape one arm around
so protectively.

RENÉE ASHLEY

(b. 1949)

∽

She is the author of three volumes of poetry. Her novel, Someplace Like This, *was published in 2003. She is on the faculty of Fairleigh Dickinson University's M.F.A. in Creative Writing program.*

Entertaining the Angel

She won't eat; even the sweetest, most translucent fruits,
    their glittering liquors, repel her. And she's not
built for dancing. Unworldly, she drifts, evanescent
    above my slick floor, my disheveled bed; she whispers
I can see you. I know what you're thinking.
    Her vague arms are open and strong; she is steady,
ambitious. She is as fine as mist, and always with me.

At first, it was the tremble of her wings that sent me
    speechless, backwards, pitching towards the fall;
it was the stark cricket on her shoulder, hard, real as coal,
    screaking in her celestial ear—an angel's own dark
and crook-legged witness. No one told me she would be there,
    but, still, at the corner of my eye, peripheral and hazy:
an edge of her nebulous hem. I could not know her. And

when she spoke, I thought it was rain, I thought
    the one white birch moved nearer, I thought it was the sound
of the lank ivy growing full before my eyes. I thought
    Be not forgetful of strangers and the angel shifted—
squarely before me she planted her pearly feet in the air,
    her faint feathers were still: *I am your angel, your genius,*
your chain. I am the distance you travel. And she knew me—

all trespass, all omission—the paltry, impossible details.
    She owns me; I am her only diversion. My barnyard of fears
is her playground, my bliss her bliss. She is adamant: No
    to the honey and iris, No to the hornpipe in the riotous street,
to the slight breeze that swings up from the dense, moist
    banks of the river. I say *robin, tango, book.*
Marble. Sunset. Bread. She becomes my hours, my intimations;

she is fraught with me. I breathe her. I think
    embodiment, manifest, God. I behold her borrowed joy,
her immaculate emptiness, behold the cricket, sturdy
    on her shoulder, the dark, seemingly eyeless mote
who keens at the coil of her shimmering ear, who speaks
    through her vast, illumined mouth, whose silence
stirs the violent wind, stirs the angel herself, moves worlds.

For Brigit in Illinois

Dear Brigit,
    (Come back.) Here the quiet moon burns
like hayfire over the mountain; the lush rose,
wild as milkweed, burgeons in the dark on the roadside
where, in daylight, you saw yourself in the stark yellow eye
of the grackle. (I never really thought you'd leave.)
Now, your words, dusky as bird wings, rise; you

reckon the distance between our lives—I can hear you
thinking. (What I know is: the good sober will burns
in you like insatiable fire. You never lost it.) The leaves
in May (do you remember?) burst from their delirious twigs
    and rose
sharp as sawteeth in the generous sky. I
thought god had made his glorious point right there, outside

the body, in the visible heaven where the new green sighed
and the air shimmered like the coruscating pond. You
spoke of angels with bodies, the soul focusing its bright eye
on substance, the solace of a promised resurrection, the burning
need for the coming together again (I believed every word).
    We rose
like spirits ourselves, two souls glad of understanding—
    the leaves

about us, above us like dreams. We thought: no one ever
    really leaves.
In this life we were wrong. In this life the issue of where you
    reside
matters (I miss you—the house finch, hungry and rose-
colored, takes his thistle like alms; he is humble and strong.
    You
would like that.) Now, all around me the bright tongue of god
    unfurls and burns
—you must see it in the plains: the gold light of morning,
    the violet dusk. I

trust we still share the vivid heavens; the idea of the
    mountains, I
leave that to recall: the way they rise beneath god's feet, the
    way the leaves
that crown them catch the vast, explosive light, and burn
around and around the countless birds who live invisibly on the
    mountainsides.
(Nothing is the same. The landscape is too big without you.)
I imagine the flat land where you live: linear, predictable,
    innumerable placid rows,

inexhaustible greens, lush golds keen as the level eye of the
    grackle as he rose
and you saw yourself go with him. (We never understood the
    birds, their cold eyes
like small stones, or like glass. The ambivalent fires rage inside
    their hollow bones—you
must understand that now, the way I understand, or think I do, the
    taking leave
of a place you love and the way sorrow, its quiet shadow ebbing,
    one day subsides.)
Nothing is forever. (Come back. Tonight the night burns

in the thousand treetops and the fire leaps even from the pale
    rose, its leaves,
its fine, myriad thorns; it springs from the eyes of the dark sleeping
    birds, from the undersides
of their dark wings. You must close your eyes. Come home
    —we'll watch the red finch burn.)

The Revisionist's Dream *(I)*

Old as seawater. And the dream as large as a sea.
We dream like that. And longer than that. Wider.
And hear the sound of bleak bells like flat stone
on flat stone. We stand—our hands are empty
and the floor is steep, the floor is a deep sea
with fish like stones who call like bells. Like
brittle bells. And the song is running water.
And the water is rising.

And the prison we choose
is narrow, and we swear we never dreamed those walls.
So the way the light breaks out from the night
is how we break away, how we carry our lives
like a sack or a sadness—and we are merely river;
the water is sweet is shallow is slow but the dream
is dark and smoky, like a woman's hair let down.
It winds like that.

AUGUST KLEINZAHLER

(b. 1949)

∞

*Born in Jersey City, he is the author of nine collections of poetry and the
recipient of awards from the General Electric Foundation, The Guggenheim
Foundation, the Lila Wallace-Readers' Digest Fund, and an Award in
Literature from the American Academy of Arts and Letters.*

Storm Over Hackensack

This angry bruise about to burst
on City Hall
will spend itself fast
so fluid and heat may build up again.

But for a moment the light
downtown
        belongs someplace else,
not here
or any town close.

Look at the shoppers, how palpable
and bright
against gathering dark
like storied figures in stereoscope.

This is the gods' perpetual light:
    clarity
    jeopardy
        change.

The Strange Hours Travelers Keep

The markets never rest
Always they are somewhere in agitation
Pork bellies, titanium, winter wheat
Electromagnetic ether peppered with photons
Treasure spewing from Unisys A-15 J mainframes
Across the firmament
Soundlessly among the thunderheads and passenger jets
As they make their nightlong journeys
Across the oceans and steppes

Nebulae, incandescent frog spawn of information
Trembling in the claw of Scorpio
Not an instant, then shooting away
Like an enormous cloud of starlings

Garbage scows move slowly down the estuary
The lights of the airport pulse in morning darkness
Food trucks, propane, tortured hearts
The reticent epistemologist parks
Gets out, checks the curb, reparks
Thunder of jets
Peristalsis of great capitals

How pretty in her tartan scarf
Her ruminative frown
Ambiguity and Reason
Locked in a slow, ferocious tango
Of if not, why not

JAMES RICHARDSON

(b. 1950)

∞

His most recent books are Interglacial: New and Selected Poems *and*
Aphorisms and Vectors: Aphorisms and Ten-Second Essays. *He teaches at*
Princeton University.

Another End of the World

Here in the last minutes, the very end of the world,
someone's tightening a screw thinner than an eyelash,
someone with slim wrists is straightening flowers,
someone is starting a slow, cloud-like settling
into a love longer than the world,
and someone's playing chess. Chess!
Some can't believe how little time is left,
some have been counting down the seconds
in pennies, all their lives. And one has realized
this day was made for him, seeing nothing
he had to do needs to be done,
and whistles, hands in pockets. This is how the world begins.

Anyway

The way an acre of starlings towers and pours
rapidly through itself, a slipping knot,
landing so few feet down the furrows (the whole skywriting
like a secret no one knows they have given away)
is one of those breathtaking wastes
(sun and the seeds they feed on being others)
in which something senseless, even selfish, absurdly magnified,
becomes grandeur (love is another).
Sometimes the flock, banking in unison,
vanishes an instant, like a sheet of paper edge-on
(a secret, anyway, is the illusion
confessing it would make a difference).
I watched this happen once—two seconds, hours—
till I understood no kindness, not a shadow or stone.
And they did not come back,
though I waited all evening (and it was you
I waited for). Though the sky turned black.

PETER MURPHY

(b. 1950)

∞

Widely published poet, directs the annual writer's conference held each January in Cape May.

The Painters

for Sonya

You were surprised to find me in the basement
when you came down to do laundry.
I was hiding from the painters and the heat
lying on the floor with my hands
behind my head, thinking of nothing.
I saw you look out a window at the gritty knees
and splattered shoes of the outside crew.
And we both could hear the inside men
upstairs moving their rollers up and down
against the walls.
You hesitated, then put down your dirty work
and joined me on that floor.
How pleased we were by this—the busy men
outside moving ladders, tying back bushes
and trees, and above us, the placing
of drop-cloths on the furniture—so much
going on around us and soon even our cutoffs
were too much to wear.

When the heat went down we went upstairs
to the new walls of our old surroundings.
Our own love-sweat mixed with the smell
of the paint. It was a place we left
not long ago and had come back to,
but better than we remembered.
We didn't know then that our daughter
was conceived, how the mixing of liquids
inside you could produce such brightness.
And outside, the foreman waited for us
in his truck, taking care of invoices,
figuring out his next job, estimates
for the future.

The Truth

after Idries Shah

1.

Everything I say is a lie,
I tell my students.
Do you believe me?

Of course, they reply.

2.

He was willing to sell you the truth,
his sign said, but you had to be willing
to pay a million dollars a word—

How can you charge so much?
the king protested.

Haven't you noticed, Nasrudin replied,
the scarcity of an item determines its cost?

3.

My computer pauses to tell me
it is "Saving 'Truth'."

Aren't we all, I say aloud.
No one is using it.

4.

The night the king decreed that liars must be hanged
Nasrudin left the city to return
when the first rooster flew into the rosy dawn,
and the sun cockled above the blossoming lemon tree.

Where are you going? the soldiers asked the darting
madman, whose screams awoke the sleeping guard
within them.

I am going to be hanged!

That can't be true said the king,
he's lying. But, said an underling,
if we hang him he'd be telling the truth.

And so they quibbled on that bridge
while Nasrudin danced around the gallows
urging them to hurry up, urging them
to take their time, to be careful
to merge all the right distinctions.

PAUL MULDOON

(b. 1951)

∞

Born in Northern Ireland. His most recent books are Poems 1968–1998
(2001) and Moy Sand and Gravel *(2002), which received the Pulitzer Prize
for poetry in 2003. He teaches at Princeton University.*

Why Brownlee Left

Why Brownlee left, and where he went,
Is a mystery even now.
For if a man should have been content
It was him; two acres of barley,
One of potatoes, four bullocks,
A milker, a slated farmhouse.
He was last seen going out to plough
On a March morning, bright and early.

By noon Brownlee was famous;
They had found all abandoned, with
The last rig unbroken, his pair of black
Horses, like man and wife,
Shifting their weight from foot to
Foot, and gazing into the future.

Hedgehog

The snail moves like a
Hovercraft, held up by a
Rubber cushion of itself,
Sharing its secret

With the hedgehog. The hedgehog
Shares its secret with no one.
We say, Hedgehog, come out
Of yourself and we will love you.

We mean no harm. We want
Only to listen to what
You have to say. We want
Your answers to our questions.

Away, keeping itself to itself.
We wonder what a hedgehog
Has to hide, why it so distrusts.

We forget the god
Under this crown of thorns.
We forget that never again
Will a god trust in the world.

Anseo

When the Master was calling the roll
At the primary school in Collegelands,
You were meant to call back *Anseo*
And raise your hand
As your name occurred.
Anseo, meaning here, here and now,
All present and correct,
Was the first word of Irish I spoke.
The last name on the ledger
Belonged to Joseph Mary Plunkett Ward
And was followed, as often as not,
By silence, knowing looks,
A nod and a wink, the Master's droll
'And where's our little Ward-of-court?'

I remember the first time he came back
The Master had sent him out
Along the hedges
To weigh up for himself and cut
A stick with which he would be beaten.
After a while, nothing was spoken;
He would arrive as a matter of course
With an ash-plant, a salley-rod.
Or, finally, the hazel-wand
He had whittled down to a whip-lash,
Its twist of red and yellow lacquers
Sanded and polished,
And altogether so delicately wrought
That he had engraved his initials on it.

I last met Joseph Mary Plunkett Ward
In a pub just over the Irish border.
He was living in the open,
In a secret camp
On the other side of the mountain.
He was fighting for Ireland,
Making things happen.
And he told me, Joe Ward,
Of how he had risen through the ranks
To Quartermaster, Commandant:
How every morning at parade
His volunteers would call back *Anseo*
And raise their hands
As their names occurred.

The Loaf

When I put my finger to the hole they've cut for a dimmer switch
in a wall of plaster stiffened with horsehair
it seems I've scratched a two-hundred-year-old itch

with a pink and a pink and a pinkie-pick.

When I put my ear to the hole I'm suddenly aware
of spades and shovels turning up the gain
all the way from Raritan to the Delaware

with a clink and a clink and a clinky-click

When I put my nose to the hole I smell the flood-plain
of the canal after a hurricane
and the spots of green grass where thousands of Irish have lain

with a stink and a stink and a stinky-stick.

When I put my eye to the hole I see one holding horsedung to the
    rain
in the hope, indeed, indeed,
of washing out a few whole ears of grain

with a wink and a wink and a winkie-wick

And when I do at last succeed
on putting my mouth to the horsehair-fringed niche
I can taste the small loaf of bread he baked from that whole seed.

with a link and a link and a linky-lick.

CATHERINE DOTY
(b. 1952)

∽

Born in Paterson, a graduate of the Iowa Writer's Workshop. Her first collection of poetry is Momentum *(2004). She lives in Boonton.*

"For May Is the Month of Our Mother"

When jump ropes smacked the softening tar
we took turns taking Mary home. She was white
with a blue screw-off bottom, supplicant hands,
and a rosary rattled inside as she swung in our book bags.
After supper is good for some, Sister Michael said,
*or before bed. If you pray the rosary, Communism
will fall.* When my turn alphabetically came for Mary,
I rattled her the two blocks up the hill,
but Catholic in our family was for kids, and Communism
was a word, not a stick or stone. My mother was tired,
my father was going to hell, I wasn't up to fifty Hail Mary's
alone, but I couldn't just dump Mary there on my cluttered dresser
like a glowing, white, wimpled bottle of shampoo
while I climbed the catalpa tree or played pies with the others,
so I set her down on our suitcase-shaped Victrola,
and put on Mom's Perry Como *Ave Maria.*
Mary stood on her snake with her begging arms out, glowing.
The sky in the window grew orange, the breeze carried lilacs.
Next, I played Nelson Eddy, *Ave Maria.* Her one-inch face
held too much sadness to bear. To cheer her up,
I played *Rum and Coca-Cola,* The Andrews Sisters, and our souls
were so open from all that *ave maria* that we threw ourselves

into the rhythm, and jumped on the bed, and I beat Mary
like a maraca in my palm, her burden of black beads clacking
thick and loud, until one slap too many cracked her right in half,
and her beads flung themselves to the floor, where they lay
like intestines. I learned then to use something right
or leave it alone. No, I didn't. I learned *twelve-inch Virgin,*
polystyrene, luminous ivory, black beads in screw-off bottom
ran $4.95, or twenty weeks of allowance.
I learned too that Mary was real to crack like that,
and I saved a splinter of her shattered gown
and I know she is patron Saint of the spring-cracked mind,
and mother of all who aspire to glow in the dark.

Momentum

Your friends won't try to talk you out of the barrel,
or your brag to go first, which has nothing to do with bravery.
And you're so hungry to earn their love you forget
to claim first your, perhaps, last look at this mountain—
crab apples hanging sour in the sun, abandoned Buick,
a favorite place to play, dismantled and weathered
and delicate as a voting booth. Instead you dive straight away
and head-first into darkness, the steel drum that dusts you,
like a chicken part, with rust. Looking out, there's nothing
to see of your friends but their calves, which are scabby,
and below them the filthy sneakers, shifting, shifting,
every foot aching to kick you off this cliff.
Their faces, you know, are blank with anticipation,
the look you see when they watch tv eating popcorn.
They're already talking about you as if you're gone,
as if you boarded a bus and roared off out of earshot,
when one foot flashes forward and launches you.

You know as you feel that first solid slam you are lost.
The barrel changes shape with each crash to earth,
as you will later, assuming and losing lives, but this
is so true now: ankles flayed to the bone, cracked ribs
and crushed mint, the brittle, pissy sumac. Right now
the pin oaks are popping in their sockets, the hillside
wears your shoes, clouds pleat and buck. You know, of course,
that no one's going second, and friends who tell this story
will use the word *idiot,* rolling their hands in the air,
but you know you know what your life is for now and rise up,
and just about scalp yourself on that tree limb above you,
another thing you couldn't possibly know was coming,
another which, like your first breath, was not your idea.

GRETNA WILKINSON

(b. 1952)

∞

Born and raised in Guyana, she began her career as a missionary teacher in the jungles there. She wrote her doctoral dissertation at Drew University on the poetry of Gwendolyn Brooks. She currently directs the creative writing program at Red Bank Regional High School.

The Amen Corner

Sister Baines almost derailed
my soul when I was nine.
In a voice that could turn
brimstone to sleet
she would boom:
    amen after *amen*
whenever the preacher said
something righteous.
Such desecration of the alphabet
nearly ruined my conviction
that *A* belonged to that first fruit
on Eve's grocery list

One Sunday, I sat in
the ancient pew
behind her ancient self
waiting to send men
to their rightful place
between L and N

Sure enough she bellowed
  aaamen
sure enough I followed
  beewomen
then waited for someone to proclaim
  ceechildren
return righteousness to the abc's

A holy hush descended
the somber preacher's glare
made my hair unkink itself.
I thought Jesus would come
any minute and fix me
like he did those money changers
in the temple

The preacher ended his sermon
gave the altar call
beckoned me to come forward
give my heart to the Lord.
So I did

I knelt at the altar
gave my heart to Jesus right quick.
Within seconds I was saved
with one new thing to worry about
  What if Adam had named the roach, fish
  Or the elephant, worm
  And should I ask Jesus
  To make Sister Baines
  Say her amens softly?

JOE WEIL

(b. 1958)

∞

Author of a number of poetry books, and celebrated for his poems praising the hopeless. He is the co-director of the Barron Arts Center, Poetry.

Bay Way, Elizabeth, Six A.M., EST

Early morning, Bay Way.
I walk upwind from the oil tank herds,
enter the same disquieting stillness
I remember from thirty years ago,
watching my father sleep off a double shift:

the unsteady rise and fall of his chest,
his work uniform still on, covered in paper dust,
old god monster of my childhood.

And now this neighborhood rises and falls,
its exhalations a war between smells:
honeysuckle and dog shit,
bus fumes and babka bread.

I've copped a Times and a
coffee regular to go.
The cup warms my hand, feels
like fresh laundered flannel.
Who wants this day to begin?

The piano store's metal eyelid
is still closed.
Mr. Gerdung dusts the Baby Grand,
chases out the kids who come to touch its keys.
Their parents don't do right, he says.
Their parents don't buy pianos.
Just one accordion student left,
and he's lazy, without talent.

The wife standing next to Vladimir Horowitz
in a photograph from 1962 is dead
ten years come May—
the same dead wife, the same unsold piano.
Usually, Mr. Gerdung opens early.
I listen to his stories and he lets me play,
His words are a ritual of loss.

Sycamore, Sweet Gum, Swamp Maple
line the streets, their roots
pushing the sidewalks up and out.
Old Polish grandmothers who scrubbed these walks
on hands and knees are dying.
Their names bloom in the obituaries,
attached to Simmons' and Singer's
long closed plants.

At the corner of Bay Way ave,
a bus lets out a flock of Haitian nurses,
fresh from the all night shift in the burbs.
Their soft laughter,
their warm, bubbling patois
is more beautiful to me
than the sound of ocean waves.

Pray God such voices
surround me in my last sleep.
Lonely and happy to be alone,
here, in Bay Way, Elizabeth.

Morning at the Elizabeth Arch

The winos rise as beautiful as deer.
Look how they stagger from their sleep
As if the morning were a river
Against which they contend.

They turn in the mind,
they turn
beyond the human order.

One scratches his head and yawns.
Another rakes a hand
through slick mats of thinning hair.
They blink and the street litter moves
its slow, liturgical way.
A third falls back
bracing himself on an arm.

At river's edge, the deer stand poised.
One breaks the spell of his reflection with a hoof
and, struggling, begins to cross.

RICH YOUMANS

(b. 1960)

∽

Rich Youmans has had his haiku, haibun, and related essays published internationally in various literary journals and anthologies. He authored Shadow Lines *with Maggie Chula, a book of "linked haibun" that won a Merit Book Award from the Haiku Society of America. He is also the editor, with Frank Finale, of* Under a Gull's Wing: Poems and Photographs of the Jersey Shore.

Ice Storm

All morning, the winter sky pressed down on us. The day out Ann and I had promised ourselves—the walk through woods, the climb up Bowman's Hill until the valley spread before us—had been lost to clouds and storm warnings, a day without horizons. Across the back lawn, apple trees raised their limbs as if in vain pleading. Dispirited, unable to fill the yawn of time facing us, Ann and I wandered through the rooms of our cottage, retracing each other's footsteps. I thought of chores—letters to be written, tile to be caulked, shelves to be hung—and did nothing. I turned on lights, turned them off; made coffee, let it grow cold. I flipped through cable channels, caught bits of bad movies and old sitcoms, canned laughter. I felt as if I were falling through the day, unable to hold onto a single idea. Ann asked about lunch, television, the weather; my silence buzzed like the dial tone after a friend had hung up. She finally retreated to the office and closed the door. I tried to read; sentences wandered back into themselves, thoughts bumped against the low sky. Late afternoon the rain began, and within an hour the windows had become crazed with ice. Tired of my own uselessness, I fell asleep.

shadows seep
deep into ice
—until the moon

Ann woke me in darkness. "It's stopped," she said, her voice soft.
"Come outside." We dressed in our heavy coats and boots, our
scarves and leather gloves. Together we entered a changed world.
Stars cascaded in endless geometries. Tree limbs had become arteries
of silver light; with each wind their branches clicked among them-
selves, as if amazed at their new circumstance. Ann and I walked
carefully onto the driveway's sheen, surrounded by starlight, moon-
light, light years; with only a few steps our cottage seemed miles
away. Surrounded by her scarf and woolen cap, Ann's small oval face
peered out at the trees as if seeing them for the first time, and I fell in
love with her all over again. Above us, icicles ran along phone wires
like the waves of beating hearts; I thought of all the voices, each with
variations on the same basic question: Are you all right? Wind rose,
branches clicked; in the distance, bright chimes gave sound to the
stars. I shouted Ann's name, just to see my white breath give it shape.
She laughed and squeezed my hand, and together we walked out into
the night, holding each other to keep from falling.

TIMOTHY LIU

(b. 1965)

∞

His first book of poems, Vox Angelica *(Alice James, 1992) received the Norma Farber First Book Award from the Poetry Society of America. Forthcoming:* Of Thee I Sing *(U. of California, 2004), and* For Dust Thou Art *(SIU, 2005). Liu has lived in Hoboken since 1998.*

Walking Alone at Ocean's Edge

And the bottle washes up. Nor cruelly spoken where a blindman
    walks
tapping code. Metronomic dawn striking ashen claves where you are
an occidental ghost steaming up the sewer grates. As paramedic
    nights

tongued their way through asphalt hot from long-gone suns—
    ambition
armored in its coat of flies. Tomorrow we die. And so on. Impenitent
remarks whip-cracking into fanfare shriek. The hullabaloo of you

like spilled Shiraz. What parrots sundry thoughts, disrobed as we are
in borrowed garb? The AC fan-belt working loose. Childhood a field
of flood-swept corn where funnel clouds tore a hayloft off its hinges.

And so to roadside woods our nakedness has fled. As operatic
    registers
rope-in herds of bucking steer more sturdy than our unsteady voices
crashing against those foghorned shores in the jetsam time maroons.

Next Day

Between the cycles of wash and rinse, a song
about to be sung, all ears lulled by a radio
while toddlers teethe on disposable pens,
while lovers spill speed across the stones
of a glassed-in vivarium, lepidoptera at rest,
in flight, in dreams, each caught in a storm
of juvenile chatroom cyber smut soaking up
chronic carpal tunnel pixel by pixel, hypnotic
pre-dawn infomercial drone in exchange for
flat TV and digitized sound, our solitudes
wired into subterranean optic lines, decrypted
surge-protected codes cruising anonymous
glass abuzz with neon glow and embryonic
lexia languishing on a music stand, marginal
notes scribbled-out below the staff, below
the institutional clock face masking hours
in that brownout run ariot, your appetite
camouflaged in grunt fatigues dirtied-up
at the knees, a song about to be sung, daisy-
chained anxieties now horse-drawn through
a gas-lit park where the dread of connubial
bliss and minuscule tectonic shifts delivered
a tremor through the family skating rink—

MATTHEW SPANO

(b. 1967)

∽

A Ph.D. in Comparative Literature from Rutgers University, he has published haiku regularly for the last ten years in the leading journals. His work has appeared in Modern Haiku, Frogpond, The Piedmont Literary Review, *and* Cicada.

March

March wind jumbles
snowflakes with cherry blossoms—
a crow's unanswered call

Scenic

scenic overlook—
buttercups peek through the cracks
in the viewfinder's base

Unruly

unruly bluebells
in a school bus chassis
rusting in a field

Tropical

tropical fish tank—
fingerprint smudges
on the "Do Not Touch" sign

Through

through the telescope—
the darkness behind Saturn,
the smell of burning leaves

BJ WARD

(b. 1967)

∞

Lives and teaches in Warren County. His third book of poetry, Gravedigger's
Birthday, *was released in 2002 by North Atlantic Books (Berkeley, CA). His
work has appeared in* Poetry, TriQuarterly, *and* Mid-American Review.

Roy Orbison's Last Three Notes

12 mph over the speed limit on Route 80, I realize
the way I know the exact size of my bones
is the way I know I am the only one
in America listening to Roy Orbison
singing "Blue Bayou" at this precise moment,
and I feel sorry for everyone else.
Do they realize they are missing
his third from last note?—*Bluuuueee*—
and how it becomes a giant mouth I'm driving into—
"Bay"—pronounced *bi*—becomes the finger
pointing back—*biiiiiiii*—and all the sealed up cars
greasing along this dirty, pot-holed clavicle of New Jersey
don't know this "you"—constant as my exhaust smoke—
yooooouuuu—and the beats underneath, more insistent
than the landlord knocking on the door—horns, drums, guitar, bass—
my Toyota Corolla is now one serious vehicle,
and the band and I are all alone, filling it up—
Roy and me in our cool sunglasses up front
and his musicians barely fitting their instruments in the back,
driving into the blue—bom bom bom—pulling ahead
of the pollution faster than New Jersey can spit it out—

Bye—boom bom—his leggy background singers must be jammed
in the trunk because suddenly I hear them and suddenly
we are Odysseus and his boys bringing the Sirens with us,
and the cassette player is our black box
containing all essential details in case we don't make it,
but I know we're going to make it
because Roy Orbison turns to me
and says, like the President says to his top general
after a war has been won, or like Morgan Earp
on his deathbed said to Wyatt when vengeance
was up to him, or like Gretchen Honecker
said when I knew I was about to get my first kiss,
Roy turns to me and says, *"You—"*

The Star-Ledger

287 was the long road to the newspaper plant
    my black-handed father would ride beneath
the weight of a night sky.
    A father who works the night shift
knows that weight, how it accumulates from within
    when his mistakes and debt
begin to press on his children and wife.
    And so went his life—

If the stars spelled something real,
    they might spell the equation
that my father never mastered—
    the news just ran through his hands
and what slid there left the black residue
    of the world's doings, pressed knowledge
that read like misaligned tea leaves in his hardening palms,
    and in his life line and heart line and other lines
that would normally speak a fortune,
    the night just accumulated itself—
a little sky he would spread over us
    when the world redelivered him in the morning.

COPYRIGHTS, PERMISSIONS, & ACKNOWLEDGMENTS

MADELINE TIGER – "Bird Song" and "Learning to Read Sky" by Madeline Tiger from *Birds of Sorrow and Joy: New and Selected Poems 1970–2000* (Marsh Hawk Press). Copyright © 2003 by Madeline Tiger. Reprinted by permission of the author.

BJ WARD – "Roy Orbison's Last Three Notes" and *"The Star-Ledger"* by BJ Ward from *Gravedigger's Birthday* (North Atlantic Books). Copyright © 2002 by BJ Ward. *"The Star-Ledger"* first appeared in *Poetry,* February, 1999. Reprinted by permission of the author.

JOE WEIL – "Bay Way, Elizabeth, Six A.M., EST" and "Morning at the Elizabeth Arch" by Joe Weil from *Ode to Elizabeth and Other Poems* (Black Swan Press). Copyright © 1994 by Joe Weil. Reprinted by permission of the author.

THEODORE WEISS – "The Fire at Alexandria" by Theodore Weiss from *From Princeton One Autumn Afternoon: The Collected Poems of Theodore Weiss, 1950–1986* (Macmillan). Copyright © 1987 by Theodore Weiss. Reprinted by permission of Renée Weiss.

RICHARD WILBUR – "Advice to a Prophet" and "Jorge Guillén: The Horses" by Richard Wilbur from *Advice to a Prophet and other Poems.* Copyright © 1959 and renewed 1987 by Richard Wilbur. Reprinted by permission of Harcourt, Inc. "Love Calls Us to the Things of This World" by Richard Wilbur from *Things of This World.* Copyright © 1956 and renewed 1984 by Richard Wilbur. Reprinted by permission of Harcourt, Inc.

GRETNA WILKINSON – "The Amen Corner" by Gretna Wilkinson. Copyright © 2005 by Gretna Wilkinson. Printed by permission of the author.

C. K. WILLIAMS – "Invisible Mending" by C. K. Williams from *Repair* (Farrar, Straus and Giroux). Copyright © 1999 by C. K. Williams. "Night" by C. K. Williams from *The Singing* (Farrar, Straus and Giroux). Copyright © 2003 by C. K. Williams. Reprinted by permission of the author.

WILLIAM CARLOS WILLIAMS – "Danse Russe," "Spring and All," and "To Waken an Old Lady" by William Carlos Williams from *Collected Poems: 1909–1939, Volume I.* Copyright © 1938 by New Directions Publishing Corp. "The Dance (In Brueghel's)" by William Carlos Williams from *Collected Poems 1939–1962, Volume II.* Copyright © 1944 by William Carlos Williams. All of the above are reprinted by permission of New Directions Publishing Corp.

RICH YOUMANS – "Ice Storm" by Rich Youmans originally appeared in *Paterson Literary Review.* Copyright © 2005 by Rich Youmans. Reprinted by permission of the author.

DANIEL ZIMMERMAN – "Last Breath" by Daniel Zimmerman. Copyright © 2005 by Daniel Zimmerman. Printed by permission of the author.

SANDER ZULAUF – "Elegy for Wally" and "Where Time Goes" by Sander Zulauf originally appeared in *5AM.* Copyright © 2003 by Sander Zulauf. "Jersey Lightning" by Sander Zulauf from *Succasunna New Jersey* (Breaking Point, Inc.). Copyright © 1987 by Sander Zulauf. Reprinted by permission of the author.

INDEX